Other Bible in Dialogue publications

The Gospel of Matthew in Dialogue
Ed G. Wallen

Additional titles in preparation

The
Gospel
of
Mark
in Dialogue

ED G. WALLEN

WESTBOW
P R E S S®
A DIVISION OF THOMAS NELSON
& ZONDERVAN

New Revised Standard Version Bible, copyright © 1989, Division of
Christian Education of the National Council of the Churches of Christ in
the United States of America. Used by permission. All rights reserved.

WestBow Press books may be ordered through booksellers or by contacting:

WestBow Press
A Division of Thomas Nelson & Zondervan
1663 Liberty Drive
Bloomington, IN 47403
www.westbowpress.com
1 (866) 928-1240

Because of the dynamic nature of the Internet, any web addresses or links contained in
this book may have changed since publication and may no longer be valid. The views
expressed in this work are solely those of the author and do not necessarily reflect the
views of the publisher, and the publisher hereby disclaims any responsibility for them.

Any people depicted in stock imagery provided by Thinkstock are models,
and such images are being used for illustrative purposes only.
Certain stock imagery © Thinkstock.

ISBN: 978-1-5127-0934-6 (sc)
ISBN: 978-1-5127-0935-3 (hc)
ISBN: 978-1-5127-0933-9 (e)

Library of Congress Control Number: 2015913825

Print information available on the last page.

WestBow Press rev. date: 10/29/2015

Contents

Abbreviations and Terms used in the Bible in Dialogue

Apoc	Apocrypha
B in D	Bible in Dialogue
b.	born
BCE	Before the Common Era (= BC)
ca	circa (about)
CE	Common Era (=AD)
CEB	Common English Bible (2011)
cf.	compare with
Ch, chs	Chapter, chapters
CMS	*The Chicago Manual of Style, Fifteenth Edition*
CWMS	*The Christian Writer's Manual of Style*
D	Deuteronomic or Deuteronomistic source (of Torah)
d.	died
E	Elohist or Elohistic source (of Torah)
Ecclus	Ecclesiasticus
e.g.	for example
Esd	Esdras
etc.	and so on
Gk	Septuagint, Greek version of the Old Testament
Heb	Hebrew of the consonantal Masoretic Text of the OT
i.e.	*id est,* that is
J	Jahwist or Yahwist source (of Torah)
Josephus	Flavius Josephus (Jewish historian about 37 to 95 CE)
KJV	King James Version of the Bible (1611)

LXX	Septuagint, the oldest translation of the OT into Greek
M	One hundred and fifty verses on the sayings of Jesus only found in Matthew and not available in Mark and Luke
Macc	The book(s) of the Maccabees
Ms(s)	Manuscript(s)
MT	The Hebrew of the pointed Masoretic Text of the OT
NIV	New International Version (1973)
NRSV	New Revised Standard Version of the Bible (1989)
NT	New Testament
OT	Old Testament, Hebrew Bible
P	Priestly source (of Torah)
Q	Q_1 the earliest writings about Jesus of Nazareth compiled about the mid 50's CE. Q_2 compiled in the late 60 or early 70s. Q_3 The smallest collection of the Gospel of Q compiled about 80 CE
Q Ms(s)	Manuscript(s) found at Qumran by the Dead Sea.
RSV	Revised Standard Version of the Bible (1946-52, 1971)
Sam	Samaritan Hebrew text of the OT
Syr	Syriac Version of the OT
Syr H	Syriac Version of Origen's Hexapla
Tg	Targum, Aramaic translation of Hebrew Bible
NJPS	New Jewish Publication Society, the Tanakh (1999)
TNIV	Today's New International Version (2002, 2004)
Vg	Vulgate, Latin Version of the OT
Webster's	*Merriam-Webster's Collegiate Dictionary, Eleventh Edition*
Wisd of Sol	Wisdom of Solomon

To the Reader

Conversing with God through study, prayer and worship has been a regular part of my faith journey. However, imagine my surprise when I heard the words one night, "Write my Word in dialogue." My immediate reaction was, "You have to be kidding." In the morning, I shared what happened with my wife and a few others who know I am not prone to hearing voices. Their response was both positive and enjoyable. The following night the same voice was heard, "Write my Word in dialogue."

So, what version should be used? Today, the reader can choose between many excellent versions of the Bible. Whenever I look at my copy of the King James Version (1611), a smile crosses my face because duct-tape holds it together. When I was in Seminary, this copy of the KJV was replaced with a Revised Standard Version (1952) because of its closeness to the Hebrew and Greek languages. When it became necessary to replace this Bible, because of use, the only RSV available was the Catholic edition. The New Revised Standard Version (1989) was selected, complete with the Apocrypha. Since the NRSV continues to be my version of choice, it was selected for the Bible in Dialogue. Placing the NRSV in a dialogue format does not change the text; it provides the reader the opportunity to experience God's Word, much as you would enjoy a dramatic production.

The traditional chapter and verse division found in the printed Bible provides an indispensable system of references, even if they do not always follow the original divisions within the text. The divisions into chapters resulted from medieval Christian scholarship, and it did not always join or separate the paragraphs, sentences and even parts of sentences in the correct manner. The reader has only to compare Genesis (Gen 7.24-8.1) in the NJPS and the NRSV to recognize the issue. "And when the waters had swelled on the earth one hundred and fifty days, God remembered Noah and all the beasts and all the cattle that were with him in the ark, and God caused a wind to blow across the earth and the waters subsided" (NJPS). "And the waters swelled on the earth for one hundred fifty days. However, God remembered Noah and all the wild animals and all the domestic animals that were with him in the ark. And God made a wind blow over the earth, and the water subsided; (the sentence continues through verse two ending following the first half of verse three in NRSV)." Readers have long understood that in the Jewish Bible the first verse of many Psalms included the subscription of the Psalm or a part, making it difficult to reference the same verse in both biblical versions. The Bible in Dialogue does not eliminate the divisions between chapters and verses; it emphasizes the stories and the voices within them.

The practice of using a period between chapter and verse (1.1) instead of a colon (1:1) is followed in the NRSV, Mt 4.4 is Matthew, chapter 4, verse 4.

Over fifty-five individuals or groups participate in the gospel of Mark in dialogue. When it applies, the meaning of a name is in square brackets with some information and scriptural references. A cast index is at the back of the B in D material to provide a page reference. The page reference for primary cast members, such as God and Jesus, is for the first time it appears in a chapter.

Italicized type in the notes indicates a quotation or word from the New Revised Standard Version (NRSV) of the passage under discussion. In addition, in scripture references to a letter (a, b, etc.) appended to a verse number indicates a clause within the verse; an additional Greek letter indicates a subdivision within the clause. When no book is named, the book under discussion is understood. When another verse is quoted, it will be shown within quotes.

Old Testament quotes or paraphrases cited in NT books will be placed in round brackets with a footnote on the location. The original cast member in the OT quote will be in the NT, with attention given to the identification of the editor when available. In Mt 5.43b, **Moses. (P)** "You shall love your neighbor and hate your enemy." In Leviticus (Lev 19.18) Moses is the speaker, according to the (P) Priestly editor.

Where do we capitalize or use the lowercase form? In the OT terms such as "Temple" (Temple at Jerusalem) and "Synagogue" are capitalized, but not in the NT. The word "gospel" will not be capitalized unless it is part of the actual title, per the *CWMS*.

The careful reader will notice in the OT the word LORD printed in small capital letters. The name "LORD" was used in the OT instead of Yahweh in most Jewish and English versions, to follow the common Jewish practice of substituting the Hebrew word "Adonai" translated as "LORD" instead of saying the name of YHWH (with no vowels). In the NT, where the LORD speaks in an OT quote, the LORD remains even if the text uses Lord.

Many biblical books resulted from a redaction process, meaning later individual writers or groups used one or more local or area traditions and edited them in developing a particular book or books of the Bible. In the Book of Genesis, at least seven editors used varied terms and traditions to identify God. Why was it important for the writers to maintain those traditions? What contribution do the individual traditions make to the total picture of the faith community? What issues moved later editors to unite the differing faith traditions? Scholars accept that many OT books, including the Psalter are a collection of many writers. However, the NT was not held to the same criteria.

Before canonization, the NT endured its share of reworking by later writers or editors to address current issues or expand upon previous statements.

In 1838, a German scholar, Christian Hermann Weisse, expressed what he believed to be the teachings of Jesus under the surface of the gospels of Matthew and Luke. These teachings or sayings are called *Quelle,* German for "the source," and are commonly known as Q. Some scholars believe the gospel of Q represents at least three collections of the sayings or teachings of Jesus and have identified them as Q_1, Q_2, and Q_3.

Q_1 was a collection of the early sayings of Jesus, compiled about the mid 50's CE. In this collection, there was no attempt to identify Jesus as the Son of God, because Jesus had something else in mind. Here, Jesus was a great teacher, who taught what the people needed to understand.

Q_2, compiled in the late 60s or early 70s, made up more than half of the gospel of Q. Q_2 presented Jesus as a teacher of great wisdom, making it easier to observe the evolution of beliefs in contrast to those of the Pharisees. This collection provides insights into the interactions between the followers of Jesus and those of John the Baptist. The Dead Sea Scrolls illuminated this issue for the reader. In addition, in Q_2 there is the introduction of an apocalyptic vision not evident in Q_1

The smallest collection of the gospel of Q was Q_3, compiled about 80 CE, after the fall of Jerusalem and close to the appearance of the gospels of Matthew and Luke. In this collection, a tone of reproach was evident for those refusing to listen and Jesus was more a Son of God than he was a wise teacher. In the B in D, the three collections of Q will be contained in brackets.

Some believe Moses or a few authors wrote the Torah in a single setting. Others believe the Bible reflected the history of God's people covering many centuries. The B in D approaches the biblical material from the position that several writers collected and interpreted both oral and written texts in light of current circumstances. While everyone may not agree on the identification of the editors or the different sources, to examine the material in this manner opens possibilities for some creative reflection upon the Word of God. Scholars mostly agree that each author or editor had a reason for what they presented. What is that reason? What is it that made their world different from ours? History, secular or religious, was written in response to an event that had altered the status quo. America is different since 9/11, and so were the biblical people after the destruction of the temple and Jerusalem in 70 CE. How did the ministries of Jesus and Paul change the Jewish and Greek communities? How did these major events and others affect the writings of the NT and the early Christian church?

Ed G. Wallen

Acknowledgments

Thanks to those at the Salem United Methodist Church, Wapakoneta, Ohio, who have used the B in D material over the past several years. Thanks to the Seek and Serve Sunday school class, the Alpha Group, the Brats in the Belfrey, the Monday Bible Study Group, the Wednesday Evening Study Group, and an Internet group called Education without Walls (Ew/oW). They each read parts of the material and enriched it with their questions and comments. Thanks to Reverends Gregory Roberts and Shawn Morris for giving faithful support, and for using this material in different settings. Special thanks to Darlene and Wayne Arnold, Don and Marj Kachelries, Kathy Latimer, Amy Miller, Stephanie Mosler and Wes McPheron for their faithfulness during this project. Thanks to Stephanie Mosler and Marguerite Wallen, for their questions, insights, and editorial skills, they are appreciated beyond words. My deepest gratitude is to my wife, Marguerite, whose love becomes more evident by her silence, when she does not agree with me, and yet she continues to encourage me. My prayer is that God will continue to bless each in this group, because they provide me with a loving climate that continues to encourage my efforts. Believe me, it makes a difference.

Names and Order of the Books of the Old and New Testament with the Apocryphal/Deuterocanonical Books

Abbreviations for the books of the Bible
Old Testament

Gen	Genesis	2 Chr	2 Chronicles	Dan	Daniel
Ex	Exodus	Ezra	Ezra	Hos	Hoses
Lev	Leviticus	Neh	Nehemiah	Joel	Joel
Num	Numbers	Esth	Esther	Am	Amos
Deut	Deuteronomy	Job	Job	Ob	Obadiah
Josh	Joshua	Ps	Psalms	Jon	Jonah
Judg	Judges	Prov	Proverbs	Mic	Micah
Ruth	Ruth	Eccl	Ecclesiastes	Nah	Nahum
1 Sam	1 Samuel	Song	Songs of Songs	Hab	Habakkuk
2 Sam	2 Samuel	Isa	Isaiah	Zeph	Zephaniah
1 Kings	1 Kings	Jer	Jeremiah	Hag	Haggai
2 Kings	2 Kings	Lam	Lamentations	Zech	Zechariah
1 Chr	1 Chronicles	Ezek	Ezekiel	Mal	Malachi

Apocryphal/Deuterocanonical Books

Tobit	Tobit	Sus	Susanna
Jdt	Judith	Bel	Bell and the Dragon
Add Esth	Addition to Esther (Gk)	1 Macc	1 Maccabees
Wis	Wisdom	2 Macc	2 Maccabees
Sir	Sirach (Ecclesiasticus)	1 Esd	1 Esdras
Bar	Baruch	Pr Man	Prayer of Manasseh
Let Jer	Letter of Jeremiah	Ps 151	Psalm 151
Song of Thr	Prayer of Azariah and	3 Macc	3 Maccabees
	The Song of the Three	2 Esd	2 Esdras
	Jews	4 Macc	4 Maccabees

New Testament

Mt	Matthew	Eph	Ephesians	Heb	Hebrews
Mk	Mark	Phil	Philippians	Jas	James
Lk	Luke	Col	Colossians	1 Pet	1 Peter
Jn	John	1 Thess	1 Thessalonians	2 Pet	2 Peter
Acts	Acts	2 Thess	2 Thessalonians	1 Jn	1 John
Rom	Romans	1 Tim	1 Timothy	2 Jn	2 John
1 Cor	1 Corinthians	2 Tim	2 Timothy	3 Jn	3 John
2 Cor	2 Corinthians	Titus	Titus	Jude	Jude
Gal	Galatians	Philem	Philemon	Rev	Revelation

The Bible – A Book of Faith

To understand the Bible requires knowledge of the differing roles Judaism, Islam, and Christianity play in history. These three religions share a common cultural background, but each has a unique interpretation concerning life upon this earth and a future kingdom. All three religions share at least parts of the OT as the basis for their faith. However, many evangelical Christians claim they must endure their existence on earth, a place of evil while preparing for the future eternal life.

While some in Judaism, accept a future life doctrine that includes rewards or punishments, it is never magnified over the present life. Judaism teaches this life is worth living for its sake, and this world and all it contains are good because God has created them. God put humanity on earth, to understand the reason for life and embrace what is good. Judaism, therefore, is concerned with the tasks, duties, and ideals of this life, assured that if this life is well lived, then the future life will take care of itself. Its concern is not salvation in a future world, but a faithful and conscious performance of the daily and often unpleasant duties of this world.

Islam teaches that God is the creator of the world and therefore everything, including wealth, ultimately belongs to God. Human beings are caretakers given the opportunity to share in and use that wealth. Muslims have always recognized that wealth was a legitimate reward for one's labors, and it also brought responsibilities, both individual and corporate. Muslims, as a way of life, recognize that all who are financially capable to pay an annual 2.5 percent wealth tax to address the needs of less fortunate members of the community.

1

For all three religions, faith is cherished and something that should express itself in a life-long conviction in a God who loves and cares for us. It is our supreme duty to know and walk with God for our entire existence. Our faith in God can only be alive and grow as we increase our knowledge of God, and only as we allow the Word of God to transform our lives into right living.

The Jewish people believe the OT (the Torah, Writings, and Prophets), and their historical traditions are the source of this knowledge. The followers of Islam believe it is in the OT and the Koran, while Christians believe both the Old and New Testaments are the sources of God's word, with an emphasis upon the NT. For all three religions, the Bible represents the thinking of many individuals, who over the centuries have raised questions about the LORD, Ali or God, and what it means to be human. The Jewish people were the first nation to see themselves as the LORD's chosen people, to know and worship God, and as messengers of his truth to all humanity. Christians, also, saw themselves as the recipient of God's love in Jesus Christ and were chosen as his messengers of that love to all humanity. The Islamic believers, also, see themselves as the chosen ones as opposed to the infidels.

The Bible, the Old and New Testaments, collected the stories of the history of the people of God, mostly Jewish and Christians. These individuals were called upon to do something, not just by the conviction that God or Jesus Christ called them, but because there was a need to confront the injustices of their day. It was about individuals who were motivated by the words of Joshua, "I hereby command you: Be strong and courageous; do not be frightened or dismayed, for the LORD your God is with you wherever you go" (Josh 1.9). The Bible contains stories about individuals called to proclaim God's will, love and ways to the world.

Therefore, it makes little difference, whether we have new truths to proclaim or old truths to reaffirm. The essential requirement for any authoritative or inspired knowledge about God must contain an historical understanding of Judaism and Christianity. Within the

Word of God is evidence of God's goodness, wisdom, and love, so maybe we can even discover how to live as the people of God today!

When we refer to the history of Judaism and Christianity, we are talking about more than a listing of events. No matter how accurate they may be, we are talking about life. We are talking about the experiences they shared, the trials they endured, in both victory and defeat. History involves a correct and complete record of all causes and effects, of all forces at work, both for good and evil, within the lives of individuals and nations. An individual's history begins long before the birth in the present conditions and continues long after a person's death as it records what changed as the result of that person's influence and actions.

The same idea goes for a nation. America's history did not just begin with the settlers who came into this land on the Mayflower ships. It began in the lives of those who visited, and the natives on the land long before the European immigrants and African slaves who came across the ocean. In the same manner, the history of Israel, Judaism and Christianity is more than a few scattered biblical accounts of events that took place. The history of the Jewish people begins with creation, as they understood it. Jewish history records their thoughts, beliefs and practices, as they grew in the knowledge of God and in their discovery of what it meant to be God's people.

It would be wise for the Christian church to convey its historical development, from the early NT period to the modern age. It would be an excellent accomplishment, but an almost impossible task given the many divisions within the Christian church. To undertake such a project would require compiling a history of the world. And if we know little about the Word of God and the development of the Christian faith, we know even less about the history of the world. Based on our lack of knowledge about the Bible, we question if we possess any sense of history?

Recently the family took a trip to Plymouth, Massachusetts, to visit of all things the famed "rock." We were surprised at how small it was, and that it was encased preventing visitors from touching it. Over the years when visitors came, they not only looked at the rock, but they chipped off a piece of it to take home. Removing a part of this historic landmark may have provided them with a souvenir, but it changed the structure for those who followed. We observed one of the Mayflower ships, and quickly noted it was not the original, but a preserved replica giving us a better perspective of what those early travelers endured during their journey. My interest in genealogy led me to the Plymouth Museum for some material on the pilgrims and their lives. One clerk was very helpful. When I told her what I wanted, she directed me to one of the books, with the comment, "This book is one of the more accurate ones that has been written." The museum had several books on that early period, written by many authors and each from a different perspective. She was telling me it was not without errors, and it contained some of the biases of the author, but it could be helpful. Since then I have found the book a wealth of information on my research of the Plymouth Colony.

Reading the Bible is like listening to the voices of many people from different places and times. They are retelling, correcting misunderstandings or inserting material that provides an historical precedent for doctrines and recorded events that must have occurred. Attend a family reunion and listen to the different stories, and you wonder if you are in the same family, because the stories are not the way you remember them. You listen to the family elders tell the oral stories about their ancestors and the old country. Now, you understand the godly priest, who wrote his story and realized not enough credit was given to Aaron or the current priest. So he added a touch of what he felt with confidence must have occurred. The victors write history, and their enemies are usually not treated with accuracy or kindness. In addition, history is rewritten to suit the needs of the present age, as facts become overlaid with commentary.

Some do not have enough faith to believe that God could reveal so much of his wisdom and truth through individuals often as fallible and biased as we are. However, to experience this with a grand result is comforting to those who do not consider ourselves perfect, and yet hope we can be to God what he is to humanity. The Bible reveals

God's glory (presence) in the lives of those who are less than perfect and who want to preserve it for others.

Some ask, "How can anyone stand up and proclaim, 'Thus says the LORD,' if the Bible is full of mistakes?" The LORD in the Bible knows the unbeliever will ask this, because the unbelieving point of view prompts the question. The response to the question must include, "Can you provide a miracle to prove that you are speaking for your God?" "Your own heart should convince you that no one has the right to treat another human being as you do. Or are you like Pharaoh, and there is no use to talk like this with you?"

The longing for a sign indicates the will of God is one of the remaining aspects of unbelief. We want an infallible church or an inerrant book to tell us exactly what we should do. Jesus said, "But this kind does not come out except by prayer and fasting" (Mt 17.21 note g). God works now as he did when the Bible was being compiled, though fallible men and women. He made us fallible so we can recognize his voice when we hear it. How did Moses know that it was the voice of the LORD speaking out of a burning bush? He knew because he understood how the LORD spoke to the great spiritual leaders in the past and was now speaking to him in the same manner. He knew because it voiced the same deep sympathy he felt for the oppressed. He knew because the voice of God called him to act on his behalf. Moses did not need a sign to prove that it was the voice of God. "I am the God of your father" (Gen 26.24). "I have observed the misery of my people" (Ex 3.7). "Come, I will send you" (Ex 3.10). The proof, that a biblical text is the word of God, is that it is the testimony of all the saints in the past, it appeals to the deepest and best in every believer's heart, and it assigns each a position in the struggle against evil and oppression.

When a prophet declared, "Thus says the LORD," sometimes he was wrong, and he was corrected by a later and more concerned decision. "You have heard that it was said in the past...But I say to you" (Mt 5.21-22). When professional clergy or priests came into positions of power and authority, it was frequently found they could confuse the will of God by requiring certain favored rituals. Some have lost their meaning but were declared to have divine origin and given more importance than matters of law, justice, mercy and faith. Every religion gathers around itself rituals that come to be as important as faith itself.

Turn on the television on any day, and you can see and hear individuals proclaiming commands in God's name. If anyone questions their validity or authority, the person making the inquiry is labeled an enemy of God. What they proclaim must be accepted, because it is the church, and God has spoken to them. We represent him on earth. However, such a conviction is only valid, if it tolerates or encourages public discussion. The Bible reveals how ancient rules and regulations, revered in the past as given by God, were in another age discussed and either affirmed or discarded in place of more meaningful precepts. The power of any ritual lies in its past benefits. It only fits that questions about their continued benefits come into question with every succeeding generation. The Bible and churches today must justify themselves to us now on grounds that they are supposed to be of divine origin.

Some have said every group interested in history has defended itself from examination by putting forth a claim to absoluteness. Our current generation is no exception. We have only advanced a little from those who worked over the material of the Bible and inserted, "Thus says the LORD" before their pet prohibitions. We will go to great lengths to avoid the intolerable examination by conscious thought. We let others do our thinking for us. Much of what was real and vital to them is today like drinking from water troughs for horses on an Internet connected world. Therefore, we not only have a responsibility, but a duty to question and discuss the will of God for us today.

Yes, the Bible is full of inspiration, wisdom, tenderness, shrewdness and devotion. It is the voice of God speaking to humanity. When and where humanity listens to the voice of God and acts, then it is God and humanity in a loving relationship.

The Cast for Mark

Andrew. [Manliness] A disciple of John the Baptist, Andrew was living in Galilee when he became Jesus' first disciple (Mt 4.18, 10.2; Jn 1.35-51). He was part of the Twelve who inquired about the end of the age (Mt 24.4-36; Mk 13.3-37; Lk 21.8-36). Andrew informed Jesus of a boy with five barley loaves and two fish, in John's account of the feeding of the five thousand (Jn 6.8). After Christ's ascension, Andrew preached in Jerusalem and died nailed to a cross in an X, later called St. Andrew's cross.

Bartimaeus. [Son of Timai] Because of his perseverance and faith, Jesus (Mk 10.46-52) healed Bartimaeus, the blind beggar of Jericho.

Blind. Jesus healed several individuals of their blindness, but Bartimaeus was the only one identified by name (Mt 9.27-36; 20.29-34; Lk 18.35-43). John recorded that Jesus healed a blind individual on the sabbath (Jn 9.1-41) and the Pharisees questioned the blind person with his parents (*see* Parents).

Bystanders. Bystanders were individuals who observed what took place, but limited their involvement (Mt 26.73; 27.40, 49; Mk 11.5).

Caiaphas. [A searcher] Joseph Caiaphas, a Sadducee, the son-in-law of Annas, was high priest of the Judeans for eighteen years (Mt 26.3, 57). At the trial of Jesus, Caiaphas presided over a meeting of some chief priests, scribes and elders to decide Jesus' fate. Determined to find Jesus guilty, he displayed a disregard for the traditional and accepted forms of Jewish law (Mt 26.57-58, 62-66; Jn 11.49, 53; 18.24; Acts 4.5).

Centurion. The title centurion identified a non-Jewish military officer in command of fifty to one hundred soldiers (Mt 8.6, 8).

Chief priests. The chief priests, an exclusive group of two hundred highborn Judeans, supervised the temple priests, the temple services, the temple treasury, and maintained the sacred vessels. They reported directly to the high priest and challenged anyone they perceived to be a danger to the temple system. They seldom acted alone, except to determine the fate of Lazarus (Jn 11.10), to strike a deal with Judas (Mt 26.14; Mk 14.10-11), to interact with Pilate (Jn 18.36; 19.15, 21) or to grant authority to Paul to persecute Christians (Acts 9.14, 21).

Christ. Christ was a title applied to the coming king expected by the Judeans, the Messiah, the Anointed One. In the NT, Christ was commonly connected with Jesus (*see* Jesus).

Crowd. The crowd represented a group or groups of Jewish people who reacted both positively and negatively to the ministry of Jesus. Outside the feeding of the four (Mt 15.32-39; Mk 8. 1-10) and five thousand (Mt 14.13 -21; Mk 6.30-44; Lk 9.10-17; Jn 6.1-15), it was not known how many people made up a crowd. Christians usually presented the crowds embracing the teachings of Jesus while the Jewish religious leaders perceived them to be indifferent and even hostile to Jesus' ministry.

David. [Beloved] David, the youngest of Jesse's eight sons, was the second and greatest king of Israel. Trained to tend sheep, yet, the LORD raised David from a low estate and placed him on the throne. David's psalms were mostly contained in book 1 of the Psalter (Pss 1-41) and quoted in the NT (Mt 22.41-46; Mk 12.36; Lk 20.42; Acts 2.34; Rom 3.4; 15.9; Heb 7.21).

Demoniac. (Gerasene) The Gerasene or Gadarene demoniac was a mentally disturbed inhabitant of the city or the surrounding district of Gadara, the capital of Perea. Matthew had Jesus curing two demoniacs (Mt 8.28-30) while Mark and Luke only mentioned one demoniac (Mk 5.1-20; Lk 8.26-39).

Demons. Belief in unclean spirits or demon possession as the cause of disease developed in late Judaism under the influence of Babylonian and Persian religions. Mark and Luke presented Jesus as someone able to deliver people from demonic oppression and Satan himself (Mk 1.23; 12.22; Lk 4.31-37; 7.33; 13.16; Acts 19.15).

Disciples. A disciple was a learner or pupil who accepted and followed a doctrine or teacher. As with Jesus, a teacher invited a disciple to become a student. The term referred to the Twelve Jesus selected to follow him. However, a majority of the times it referred to more than the Twelve (Mt 8.2; Mk 3.7; Lk 6.13; 10.1-16; 19.3 7; 6.66-67). John the Baptist had several disciples, including Andrew (Jn 1.40). The Pharisees had disciples, often identified as lawyers or scribes, whose primary responsibilities were to study the Scriptures (Mt 22.16-21).

Elders. The Elders of Israel were individuals with status or personality within the community. They conducted their business at the gates of the community (Gen 23.12; 50.7; Ex 3.15; Mt 21.23, 31, 41; 26.5; 27.4-7, 42-43).

Father. The father was the head of the family and expected honor and obedience. In the Bible, the word "father" was frequently used to describe the nature of God (Prov 3.11-12, 34; Mt 21.28; 25.8-11; Mk 9.14-29; Lk 5.11-32; 9.34-42; Heb 12.5; James 4.6; 1 Pet 5.5).

God. In the Bible, it was inappropriate to ask the question, "Did God exist?" rather the question should be, "Who was your God?" The name given to the Divine in the OT revealed the nature of the Divine and the relationship between the Divine and the people.

In the account of the burning bush, Moses hesitated to accept a task from the God of the Ancestors, the God of Abraham, the God of Isaac and the God of Jacob (Ex 3.6). A later editor (LJE) then identified God as LORD or "ha-Shem" (Ex 3.7), but the issue remained. If Moses went back to the people in Egypt and said, "The God of your ancestors has sent me," they would ask, "What was his name?" He would have to identify God as, "I AM WHO I AM" (Ex 3.14), meaning, "I cause to be what comes into existence" and "I will be with you." The LORD sent Moses back to Egypt to assure the Israelites he could deliver what he proclaimed. He then humiliated the most powerful ruler of that time and called upon the forces of nature to fulfill his will, the deliverance of the Israelites. The LORD said to the Israelites, at the consecration of the tent of meeting and the altar, "I will meet with the Israelites there, and it shall be sanctified by my glory; I will consecrate the tent of meeting and the altar; Aaron also and his sons I will consecrate, to serve me as priests. I will dwell among the Israelites, and I will be their God. And they shall know that I am the LORD their God, who brought them out of the land of Egypt that I might dwell among them; I am the LORD their God" (Ex 29.43-46).

Herod. [Son of the hero] Herod the Great (73-4 BCE) was appointed governor of Syria with the promise of a later appointment as king of Judea. The Judeans, who allied with him, received high honors, and his opposition, including members of the Sanhedrin, received bitter vengeance. He had ten wives and fifteen children, of which ten were sons, setting up an inevitable domestic struggle for the throne (Mt 2.8). His son, Herod Antipas by a Samaritan wife named Maithace, governed as Prince of Galilee and Perea (Trans-Jordan) until his death in 39 CE (Mt 14.2; Lk 9.9).

Herodians. Individuals who regarded the Herodian dynasty as the best solution to the Judean problem were Herodians. These Herodian sympathizers united forces with the Pharisees in opposing Jesus (Mt 33.15-22; Mk 3.6; 12.13-17; Lk 20.20-26).

Herodias. Herodias was the wife of Herod Antipas and the daughter of Aristobulus and Bernice. Herodias married the half-brother of her father, and they became the parents of Salome. John the Baptist denounced this marital relationship and the daughter, Salome, after a dance in vengeance demanded and received John the Baptist's head on a platter (Mt 14.3-12; Mk 6.17-29; Lk 3.19-20).

Isaiah. [The LORD is Helper] The book of Isaiah contained at least three distinct sections, from three periods and was written by at least three authors, and maybe reworked by many later editors. Isaiah (I) chapters 1-39 were mostly the work of the prophet Isaiah, who lived in Jerusalem during the eighth century BCE. Chapters 24-27 were identified as the Isaiah Apocalypse, because of its themes concerning the end of the age. Chapters 36-39 was an appendix, taken from the book of Kings, sometime around the last half of the fourth century and the early part of the second century BCE.

Many Jewish and Christian scholars agree that chapters 40–55 of Isaiah, known as Deutero-Isaiah or Second Isaiah (D-I), reflected another historical setting, the Babylonian exile of the sixth century. The author of Deutero-Isaiah was in the Babylonian exile writing to his fellow Judeans. Some believe Deutero-Isaiah may have been one of the later editors to change chapters 1-39.

Chapters 56–66, known as Trito-Isaiah (T-I), are thought to have been written by disciples of Deutero-Isaiah. This editor made sure the master's writings were brought to Judah from Babylon. Since Trito-Isaiah quoted or pointed to Deutero-Isaiah, this indicated he wrote after the exile. Later editors may have added or inserted additional material even as late as the first half of the second century BCE. There are almost a hundred quotes in the NT from the book of Isaiah.

Jairus. [He will enlighten] Jairus was the leader of a synagogue whose daughter Jesus raised from the dead (Mk 5.22; Lk 8.41).

James and John. James and his younger brother, John, sons of Zebedee, a Galilean fisherman, were disciples of Jesus. Tradition holds that their mother Salome was the sister of Mary, the mother of Jesus. James was killed by Herod Agrippa with a sword (Mt. 4.21; 10.2; 17.1; 20.22; Mk 1.19, 29; 3.17; 5.37; 9.2; 10.35, 41; 13.3; 14.33; Lk 5.10; 6.14; 8.51; 9.28, 54; Acts 1.13; 12.2).

James. (Brother of Jesus) Those who believed Mary remained a virgin suggested that James was a child of Joseph by a former marriage, or the word "brother" was loosely used and may be "cousin". He was not considered a believer during Jesus' lifetime (Mt 13-57; Lk 7.20-21; Jn 2.12; 7.3, 10). After Jesus' death, James became the leader of the Jewish Christian church at Jerusalem (Acts 12.17; 15.4-34; 21.18, 19; Gal 2.1-10). He was called James the Just because of his piety and honesty. He was beheaded in 60 CE.

Jesus. [Jehovah is Salvation] Joseph was told that Mary, his wife, was to have a son, and he should name him Jesus (Mt 1.21). During his teaching and healing ministry in Palestine, Jesus received other names including: Advocate (Jn 14.15-16), Prophet (Jn 1.21; 614; 7.40), Messiah (Jn 1.41; 4.25), Christ (Mt 16.16), Anointed One, Judge (Jn 12.47-49), Rabbi (Jn 1.38, 49; 6.25; 9.2), Galilean (Mk 1.9, 14; 4.15), Master, Teacher (Mt 5.21-22), Son of Man (Mk 2.10; Jn 5.27), John the Baptist, Elijah, Jeremiah, Mediator, King of Israel (Mk 11.9-10; Lk 19 38; Jn 1.49; 12.13) High Priest (Heb 10.21-25), Servant of God (Jn 1,49), Lamb of God (Jn 1.29, 36, 41), Light of the World (Jn 6.16-21; 8.12), Son of David, Judge, Holy One of God, Lord (Mt 28.20), Savior (Jn 4.42), King, Word (Logos) (Jn 1.1-3; Heb 1.1-2), Son of God (Mk 14.61-64; Jn 5.18; 10.33), and the Good Shepherd (Mk 14.7; Jn 10.15-18; 13.37-38; 15.13). These names all described his unique relationship with God and raised the messianic expectations of the people. The NT contained the story of Jesus' life, death, and resurrection, as he became the founder of the Christian faith.

Jesus' Brothers. John mentioned Jesus' brothers in his gospel (Jn 2.12; 7.3-10), yet, Matthew and Mark identifed them by name (Mt 13.55-56; Mk 6.3). It appeared they only believed Jesus to be the

Messiah after the resurrection (Gal 1.19; Acts 12.17; 15.13-21; 1 Cor 9.5; 15.7).

John the Baptist. The Synoptic Gospels considered John the Baptist to be the forerunner of the Messiah. (Lk 1.16, 76). Jesus identified John the Baptist as Elijah (Mt 17. 10-11). When asked by the priests and Levites from Jerusalem, if he was the prophet, John responded, "No" (Jn 1.21). Early Christians regarded John the Baptist to be the prophet who was the forerunner of the Messiah. However, the Baptist's disciples considered him the final prophet who prepared the way for God himself (Lk 1.15), expressing the belief that the Messiah was the same as the "eschatological prophet."

Judas Iscariot. [Praise of the LORD] Judas, son of Simon, was not only one of the Twelve, but he was the treasurer of the group (Jn 6.71; 12.6; 13.26, 29). The word "Iscariot" may mean "man from Kerioth", a town in southern Judea, making Judas the only Judean among the Twelve. His name was always listed, "the one who betrayed Jesus." According to Matthew, after the betrayal of Jesus, Judas threw the money down in the temple and then hung himself (Mk 27.3-10). However, Luke in Acts recorded a different account (Acts 1.18-19) where Judas bought a field with the betrayal money; and falling headlong, he burst open in the middle, and all his bowels gushed out.

Leper. A leper was expected to separate himself and to cry "Unclean, unclean" as a warning to others of his condition (Deut 13.45-46). It would have been unlawful for a leper to approach anyone (Mt 8.1-4). In Luke's gospel, Jesus healed ten lepers, and only one returned to thank him (Lk 17.10-19).

LORD. The name "LORD" was used in the OT instead of Yahweh in most Jewish and English versions, to follow the common Jewish practice of substituting the Hebrew word "Adonai" translated as "LORD" instead of saying the name of YHWH (with no vowels).

LORD **God.** The designation "LORD God" or "ha-Shem" was a translation of "Yahweh" and "Elohim" indicating a unity between the Yahwist (J) and Elohist (E) traditions. Its designation was in the story of the Paradise and the fall (Gen 2-3). A variation of the two traditions was the LORD, my God.

Lord GOD. (*see* LORD God)

Man in white robe. When Mary Magdalene, Mary, and Salome entered the tomb of Jesus, in Mark's gospel (Mk 16.1-8), they were met by a young man, dressed in a white robe, who gave them a message for his disciples and Peter.

Mark. [A large hammer] - **(Mk)** John Mark was a Judean and a son of Mary, who was a leading Christian in Jerusalem. John was his Hebrew name and Mark was the Roman surname of this young companion of Paul and Barnabas, believed to be the brother of Mark's mother (Acts 13.1-5). In his early years, Mark fell out of Paul's grace (Acts 13.13; 15.38), however, he later regained Paul's trust (Col 4.10-11; Philem 24). Mark was a close companion of Peter for almost twelve years (1 Pet 5.13). Tradition has it that Mark became a bishop and a martyr and that his body was moved to Venice for burial. His gospel reflected Peter's teachings, and as the earliest and shortest of the gospels, it later became a valuable source for Matthew and Luke.

Mary Magdalene. Mary was one of the most prominent Galilean women to follow Jesus. Luke introduced her as "Mary called Magdalene, from whom seven demons had come out" (Lk 8.2). Her devotion to Jesus and his ministry was evident, as she provided for Jesus and his disciples out of her resources (Mk 15.40-41; Lk 8.3). She accompanied Jesus and his followers to Jerusalem for his final appeal to the nation (Mk 15.40; Jn 19.25), was present at the cross, came to the tomb to anoint the body (Mk 16.1; Lk 23.55-24.1), reported the empty tomb and the angel's message to the disciples (Lk 24.1-11), and met Jesus after the resurrection (Jn 20.11-18).

Mary. (the mother of Jesus) It becomes difficult to describe Mary as an historical person. Tradition holds her "as the servant of the Lord" (Lk 1.38), who became the instrument for God to visit humanity in a child born of a virgin, that he may redeem them from sin and death and lead them into his blessed kingdom. She was a devout Jewess, who lived in Nazareth. She may have been of Levite descent because of her relationship with Elizabeth. A second century writing (*Protoevangelium of James*) identified her parents as Joachim and Anna. She was engaged to Joseph, from the house of David, when she conceived. This was a shock to Joseph, but his fears were put to rest by the assurances of an angel (Mk 1.20-21).

It is not clear how early the doctrine of the virgin birth became a part of the early church, because it did not appear in the NT except in Matthew (Mt 1.23) and Luke (Lk 1.34-35), but this does not deny the possibility that Jesus was virgin born, making him unique at birth. Mary's offering at the end of her period of uncleanness of "a pair of turtledoves or two young pigeons" indicated the humble lifestyle of this new family (Lev 12.6-8). There remains little information about the childhood of Jesus and his relationship with his parents, except for their annual visit to Jerusalem during the festival of the Passover, but it was different when Jesus was twelve years of age (Lk 2.41-52).

John had Mary appearing at the beginning of Jesus' ministry at the wedding at Cana (Jn 2. 1-11). Mark had Mary and Jesus' brothers seek Jesus in order to have him return home with them. Instead of welcoming them, he told his hearers that his real relatives were those who joined him in obedience to the will of God (Mk 3.31-35). Mary appeared at the foot of the cross with the beloved disciple (Jn 19.25-27), when Jesus gave them to each other, and he took her into his home.

Mary appeared again in Acts (Acts 1.14) where she participated in a prayer meeting, following Jesus' resurrection and ascension, with the apostles and the brothers of Jesus. Legend holds that Mary died in Jerusalem (other legends that she died in Ephesus) attended by the apostles. Legend also had it that a Jewish priest, during the funeral, laid his hands on the bier to overturn it, only to discover that he could not free his hands until he had confessed faith in Mary's divine Son. After the body of Mary was placed in a new sepulcher, Jesus appeared with a band of angels, and at his command, the angels carried her into paradise.

Mary. (The sister of Martha) Mary was the sister of Martha and Lazarus of Bethany (Jn 11.1-12.2). At the death of her brother, Lazarus, she received a message from Martha of Jesus' presence and admonished Jesus for not being there (Jn 11.32). After the resurrection of Lazarus, Mary anointed the feet of Jesus while Martha served at a dinner for Jesus (Jn 12.1-8). Mark (Mk 14.3-9) had this meal in the house of Simon, the leper and that an unnamed woman anointed Jesus.

Messenger. An individual, who carried a message from its sender to the intended reader, with no other identification was the messenger (Mt 12.47; 25.6).

Messiah. (false) There were several individuals during the period before and after Jesus, who falsely claimed to be the messiah. Theudas appeared in 45 CE during the reign of Cuspius Fadus (Acts 5.36) and misled four hundred men. Later Judas the Galilean convinced people to follow him, but he was killed (Acts 5.37). In 54 CE, a Jewish Egyptian was put to death by Felix (Acts 21.38), after persuading thirty thousand people to follow him to the Mount of Olives promising that upon his command the walls of Jerusalem would fall. Then there was Simon bar Kochba whose revolt was smashed in 135 CE (Mt 24.24; Mk 13.22; Lk 21.28).

Moses.[Taken out of the water] Moses was the youngest son of Amran and Jochebed, his wife, of the tribe of Levi, the third son of Jacob. Moses was among the greatest Hebrew leaders and legislators for the Israelite people.

People. In the biblical text, there were several gatherings of people with or without additional information. Sometimes a location provided additional information, such as, people from the home of Simon the leper (Mk 14.3-9) or the home of Jairus (Mk 5.35). In other NT places, they might be identified as "crowd" (*see* Crowd) or just "people" (Mt 11.18-19; Mk 2.18; 3.21; 7.37; 14.4; Lk 7.33-34; 20.16; Jn 6.14; 7.25-42).

Peter. [A rock] Peter, also known as Simon Peter, began as a fisherman and became a "rock." Jona or Jonah was his father and Andrew was his brother. The brothers were fishermen on the Lake of Galilee and may have been in partnership with Zebedee and his two sons, James and John. Peter's brother Andrew introduced him to Jesus, and he was to become his friend, disciple, and apostle. Peter was impulsive (Mt 14.28; 17.4), tenderhearted, and affectionate (Mt 26.75; Jn 13.9; 21.15-17). He possessed spiritual insight (Jn 6.68), and yet found it difficult to understand (Mt 15.15-16), courageous and yet he denied Jesus (Mt 16.16; Jn 6.69; Mk 14.67-71), self-sacrificing and at other times self-seeking (Mt 19.27). He became the leader of the early apostles and became a miracle worker. He carried the gospel message to the Gentiles and in 61 CE traveled to Rome before Paul's release from prison. A few years later, Peter suffered martyrdom by crucifixion but pleaded to be crucified upside down.

Pharisees. The leading Jewish party or sect was the Pharisees, a group of middle class, substantial citizens, mostly devout and intelligent laity. The Pharisees' origin came be traced to when the Jewish people returned from exile. They could not follow the exclusive path of the religious leaders, and so they separated themselves. Over the centuries, they became exclusive and separated themselves from the unclean to observe the ritual purity of the Law. They believed the Law was perfect and permanent, and the purpose of life was absolute obedience. Among the Pharisees, there were elders, people older in age, scribes, who studied and interpreted the Law, and Zealots, who were ready to lay down their lives in the struggle for freedom. Some of Jesus' harshest words were directed against the hypocrisy of the Pharisees, who were his chief enemies.

Pilate. [One armed with a dart] After being tried before the Sanhedrin, Jesus was presented to Pontius Pilate, the Roman procurator of Judea (26-36 CE), to be tried and crucified (Mt 27.1-26; Mk 15.1-15; Lk 23; Jn 18.28-19.16).

Rich young ruler. The title, rich young ruler, resulted from combined information from the Synoptics. Mark called him a "rich man" (Mk 10.17-31), and Matthew called him a "young man" (Mt 19.16-30). Luke identified him as a "ruler," a member of the governing body of a synagogue (Lk18.18-30)

Sadducees. The Sadducees were the biblical fundamentalists of ancient Palestine. They were a group of conservative, aristocratic, landowning, priestly families whose lives centered on the Jerusalem temple. They insisted that a faithful believer needed to understand the Torah. They rejected what they believed to be the modern traditions of the scribes and the doctrine of the resurrection. Their fellow Judeans hated these Sadducees, because of their collaboration with Rome, their zeal for the Law and their unwillingness to address the concerns of the people. The Sadducees disappeared from Jewish history following the destruction of Jerusalem and the temple in 70 CE.

Salome. There were two women with the name Salome. The first was a Galilean follower of Jesus, probably the wife of Zebedee and the mother of James and John (cf. Mt 20.20-24; Mk 10.35-41). The second was the daughter of Herodias, who danced for Herod Antipas and his guests and requested the head of John the Baptist for payment. (Mt 14.6; Mk 6.22).

Scoffers. Scoffers responded with words of contempt or insincerity (Mt 7.21; 24.23-26; Lk 14.30; see Rom, Cor and 2 Pet).

Scribes. The Pharisees were the only group to have scribes, and they were experts in the religious law. It was also a term that gave way to the title "rabbi."

Servant girl. This individual may have been one of the slaves or servants of Caiaphas who inquired if Peter was a follower of Jesus (Mt 26.71; Mk 14.67; Lk 22.56).

Simon. [Hearing] In the NT, there are several individuals with the name Simon, beside Simon Peter. Simon the Cananaean was listed as one of the disciples. There was Simon, the sorcerer or magician, in Samaria who wanted to purchase the gifts of the Spirit from the apostles with money (Acts 8.9-24). There was Simon the healed leper in Bethany (Mt 26.6-13; Mk 14.3-9; Jn 12.1-8) who later invited Jesus to dine and where his head was anointed with oil. Luke identified this dinner host as a Pharisee who appeared to be friendly to Jesus, but who with other guests may have used this occasion to express their criticism of Jesus (Lk 7.36-50).

Soldiers. It remains unclear if the text refered to the Roman military (Mt 8.8; 27.27-29; Lk 7.8; Acts 12.4; 21.32), or if they were temple guards under the direction of the chief priest (*see* temple police). Whenever the Roman governor traveled from Caesarea to Jerusalem, it was with a cohort of soldiers (five thousand) to keep order during one of the Feasts.

Synagogue members. A Jewish synagogue was comprised of at least ten Jewish adults.

Temple singer. In late Jewish times, during the daily offering two priests with silver horns would stand behind the singing choir and at every section of the psalm there would be a pause, the priests would blow on their horns and the congregation would fall down in worship. A presenter, temple singer, or priest usually began the hymns followed by a response from the temple choir. Or, the hymn might be sung by two temple choirs, as evident in Psalm 136. This practice would be more like the responsive readings conducted in most churches today.

Tenants. In Jesus' parable of the vineyard, the landowner planted a vineyard, put a fence around it, dug a winepress in it and built a watchtower. Then he leased it to tenants while he went to another country. At harvest time, he sent his slaves to the tenants to collect his produce, but they beat one, killed another and stoned another. They also killed the landowner's son. (Mt 21.33-46).

Vineyard owner. In the parable of the vineyard, God was the owner of the vineyard, and the vineyard represented Israel. The tenants were the leaders of Judaism, and the slaves were the OT prophets. Jesus was the beloved son murdered by crucifixion. The destruction of the wicked was the destruction of the temple, and the new tenants were the apostles and the early church (Mt 21.33-36).

Witnesses. (two false) Since Jewish law required that two witnesses give testimony before putting anyone to death (Num 35.30; Deut 19-15), two false witnesses provided this testimony against Jesus (Mt 26.61).

Woman. The function and status of women in the Bible, as wives and mothers, were strongly influenced by the patriarchal form of family life. Here, a woman was not identified by name, but by region, Canaanite (Mt 15.22-27; 27.54), Samaritan (Jn 4.1-42), at the gate of the high priest (Jn 18.17), or by an illness (Mt 9.21-22).

Introduction to the Gospel of Mark

Peter, the impulsive disciple, who followed Jesus about Galilee, lived to share in the worldwide Gentile mission before meeting his death in Rome in 64 CE. His death ended the physical link between the early church and the earthly ministry of Jesus. Christianity had lost one of its greatest human documents about the life of Jesus.

The familiar stories of Jesus' words and deeds, and of his expected return, would no longer be heard from the lips of Peter. Yet, no one felt it was important to record what Peter said and his precious accounts of Jesus were in danger of being lost to the world. However, there was a young man in Rome, who had traveled with Peter for a time. When Peter preached to little companies of Roman Christians in his native Aramaic, it was Mark who stood at his side translating the words into Greek. Earlier in his youth, Mark had gone with Paul and Barnabas on their first missionary journey to Cyprus, but he had disappointed and offended Paul by withdrawing from the party when they had landed in Pamphylia and proposed to push on into the center of Asia Minor (Acts 13.13). Later as a young man, Mark traveled again to Cyprus with Barnabas. Through the years, Mark probably maintained close contact with the Christian leaders at Antioch and at Jerusalem where his mother's house had been a center for the Christian community since its beginning. It was probably as Peter's companion that Mark made his way to Rome and served as the disciple's interpreter until Peter was killed.

Mark realized at once the enormous loss the churches faced when Peter's eyewitness accounts of Jesus perished, and to preserve some of those firsthand accounts would provide comfort and instruction to the Roman believers. Since Mark had been translating Peter's sermons about Jesus, he was familiar with the message of Jesus and could write down much of what Peter said about Jesus in Galilee and in Jerusalem from personal experience only thirty years earlier.

Today, what Mark wrote down is found in the Gospel according to Mark. However, Mark probably did not call these writings a gospel, because if he had named his work, he probably would have given it Peter's name rather than his own. Yet, Christians are indebted to Mark for placing in a written form much of what Peter remembered and preached about Jesus. Mark tried to preserve faithfully what Peter told repeatedly about Jesus.

Jesus was presented as drawn to John the Baptist's preaching in the hills of Galilee, where when baptized by John, Jesus immediately possessed the Spirit of God. He was filled with a divine sense of his commission as God's anointed, to establish God's kingdom in the world. Yet, he remained silent until John's arrest and imprisonment. Then only when John's work was cut short, did Jesus preach in Galilee (Mk 1.14). Marvelous cures accompanied his preaching, and no matter where he went, there was a crowd of Galileans around him. The manner in which he dealt with the oral traditions of the Law, quickly brought Jesus into conflict with the Pharisees, and their increasing opposition before long threatened his life. After withdrawing from Galilee, two or three times, in search of security or to plan his response, Jesus informed the disciples he must go to Jerusalem in the springtime for the Feast of the Passover. He told them the journey would cost him his life, but he proclaimed God would save him and raise him up. Confused and alarmed the disciples followed him to Jerusalem, which he entered in triumph. Now for the first time he declared himself the Messiah by riding into the city as Zechariah prophesized the Messiah would enter it (Zech 9.9). Jesus boldly entered the temple and drove out of its courts the privileged dealers in sacrificial victims and moneychangers who had made it their marketplace. The Sadducees, who were in control of the temple and who profited from these abuses, on the night of the Passover had him arrested and after hasty examinations before Jewish and Roman authorities prepared him on the next morning to be executed. Up to the hour of his arrest, Jesus did not give up hope of succeeding in Jerusalem and winning the nation to his teaching of the presence of the kingdom of God on the earth (Mk 14.34-36).

The book more than once predicted his resurrection and in its completed form contained a brief account of his appearance to Mary Magdalene and Mary the Mother of James, and Salome after his burial. By the beginning of the second century, the original ending of the gospel was lost, and while two conclusions have been used in different manuscripts to complete it, the original one, probably only ten or twelve lines long, has never been restored.

Mark's gospel narrative was held in high esteem by the ancient church, when compared to the works of Matthew and Luke, and there was no more convincing or dramatic account written about the efforts of Jesus to establish the kingdom of God on earth.

Mark

Chapter 1
Activity of John the Baptist, 1.1-8
(Mt 3.1-12; Lk 3.1-20; Jn 1.6, 15, 19-28)

Mark. The beginning of the good news[a] of Jesus Christ, the Son of God.[b] **[Q₂][**²As it is written in the prophet Isaiah,[c]

LORD. "See, I am sending my messenger ahead of you,[d] who will prepare your way; [e]]

Isaiah. (D-I)(³ the voice of one crying out in the wilderness:

Messenger. 'Prepare the way of the Lord, make his paths straight,'" [f])

Mark. [Q₂][⁴ John the baptizer appeared[g] in the wilderness, proclaiming a baptism of repentance for the forgiveness of sins. ⁵And people from the whole Judean countryside and all the people of Jerusalem were going out to him, and were baptized by him in the river Jordan, confessing their sins.] ⁶Now John was clothed with camel's hair, with a leather belt around his waist, and he ate locusts and wild honey. **[Q₂][**⁷ He proclaimed,

---

a   Or *gospel*
b   Other ancient authorities lack *the Son of God*
c   Other ancient authorities read *in the prophets*
d   Gk *before your face*
e   Mal 3.1
f   Isa 40.3
g   Other ancient authorities read *John was baptizing*

John the Baptist. "The one who is more powerful than I is coming after me; I am not worthy to stoop down and untie the thong of his sandals. [8] I have baptized you with[h] water; but he will baptize you with[i] the Holy Spirit."]

Jesus' baptism, 1.9-11
(Mt 3.13-17; Lk 3.21-22; Jn 1.29-34)

Mark. [Q$_1$][[9] In those days Jesus came from Nazareth of Galilee and was baptized by John in the Jordan. [10]And just as he was coming up out of the water, he saw the heavens torn apart and the Spirit descending like a dove on him. [11] And a voice came from heaven,

God. "You are my Son, the Beloved;[j] with you I am well pleased."]

Jesus' temptation, 1.12-13
(Mt 4.1-11; Lk 4.1-13)

Mark. [Q$_3$][[12] And the Spirit immediately drove him out into the wilderness. [13] He was in the wilderness forty days, tempted by Satan; and he was with the wild beasts; and the angels waited on him.]

Beginnings of Jesus' activity in Galilee, 1.14-39
(Mt 4.12-17; Lk 4.14-15)

Mark. [14] Now after John was arrested, Jesus came to Galilee, proclaiming the good news[k] of God,[l] [15] and saying,

Jesus. "The time is fulfilled, and the kingdom of God has come near;[m] repent, and believe in the good news."[n]

---

[h] Or *in*
[i] Or *in*
[j] Or *my beloved Son*
[k] Or *gospel*
[l] Other ancient authorities read *of the kingdom*
[m] Or *is at hand*
[n] Or *gospel*

Mark. [16]As Jesus passed along the Sea of Galilee, he saw Simon and his brother Andrew casting a net into the sea—for they were fishermen. [17]And Jesus said to them,

Jesus. "Follow me and I will make you fish for people."

Mark. [18]And immediately they left their nets and followed him. [19]As he went a little farther, he saw James son of Zebedee and his brother John, who were in their boat mending the nets. [20]Immediately he called them; and they left their father Zebedee in the boat with the hired men, and followed him.

[21]They went to Capernaum; and when the sabbath came, he entered the synagogue and taught. [22]They were astounded at his teaching, for he taught them as one having authority, and not as the scribes. [23]Just then there was in their synagogue a man with an unclean spirit, [24]and he cried out,

Demoniac. "What have you to do with us, Jesus of Nazareth? Have you come to destroy us? I know who you are, the Holy One of God."

Mark. [25]But Jesus rebuked him, saying,

Jesus. "Be silent, and come out of him!"

Mark. [26]And the unclean spirit, convulsing him and crying with a loud voice, came out of him. [27]They were all amazed, and they kept on asking one another,

Synagogue members. "What is this? A new teaching—with authority! He° commands even the unclean spirits, and they obey him."

Mark. [28]At once his fame began to spread throughout the surrounding region of Galilee.

° Or *A new teaching! With authority he*

[29]As soon as they[p] left the synagogue, they entered the house of Simon and Andrew, with James and John. [30] Now Simon's mother-in-law was in bed with a fever, and they told him about her at once. [31] He came and took her by the hand and lifted her up. Then the fever left her, and she began to serve them.

[32]That evening, at sunset, they brought to him all who were sick or possessed with demons. [33]And the whole city was gathered around the door. [34] And he cured many who were sick with various diseases, and cast out many demons; and he would not permit the demons to speak, because they knew him.

[35]In the morning, while it was still very dark, he got up and went out to a deserted place, and there he prayed. [36] And Simon and his companions hunted for him. [37]When they found him, they said to him,

Peter and Disciples. "Everyone is searching for you."

Mark. [38]He answered them,

Jesus. "Let us go on to the neighboring towns, so that I may proclaim the message there also; for that is what I came out to do."

Mark. [39]And he went throughout Galilee, proclaiming the message in their synagogues and casting out demons.

Ministry and controversy, chiefly in Galilee, 1.40-9.50

Mark. [40]A leper[q] came to him begging him, and kneeling[r] he said to him,

Leper. "If you choose, you can make me clean."

---

[p] Other ancient authorities read *he*

[q] The terms *leper* and *leprosy* can refer to several diseases

[r]   Other ancient authorities lack *kneeling*

28

Mark. [41] Moved with pity,[s] Jesus[t] stretched out his hand and touched him, and said to him,

Jesus. "I do choose. Be made clean!"

Mark. [42]Immediately the leprosy[u] left him, and he was made clean. [43]After sternly warning him he sent him away at once, [44] saying to him,

Jesus. "See that you say nothing to anyone; but go, show yourself to the priest, and offer for your cleansing what Moses commanded, as a testimony to them."

Mark. [45] But he went out and began to proclaim it freely, and to spread the word, so that Jesus[v] could no longer go into a town openly, but stayed out in the country; and people came to him from every quarter.

Chapter 1 Notes
Activity of John the Baptist, 1.1-8

1: The opening sentence of Mark's gospel introduced the emphasis or focus for his book (Mk 1.1). *The good news,* the gospel, was the story of God's activity through *Jesus Christ, the Son of God (see* Jesus as the Son of God) and what Paul identified as the "power of God for salvation" (Rom 1.16). The term *good news* carried with it an association of the Hebrew word meaning "news" or "glad tidings" as used in Isaiah (Isa 40.9; 61.1) to proclaim God's deliverance. It was not until Justin Martyr (150 CE), that the term *good news* applied to the gospels with Jesus as the savior of humanity (Mk 13.10; 14.9). The combined name or title *Jesus Christ (see* Jesus as the Christ)

---

[s] Other ancient authorities read *anger*
[t] Gk *he*
[u] The terms *leper* and *leprosy* can refer to several diseases
[v] Gk *he*

was common in the writings of Paul, but it was only used as a statement of faith in the gospels (Mk 1.1; Jn 1.17). Messiah (*see* Jesus as the Messiah) in the Hebrew and *Christ* in the Greek both mean, "Anointed." Mark used the term *Christ* as the anointed to avoid a reference to Jewish nationalism and to include his Roman Christian audience. The term *son of God* was used in the OT to describe angels, divine beings (Gen 6.2; Job 38.7), or the Israelite nation (Hos 11.1) and was used once regarding the anointed king (Ps 2.7). In the Graeco-Roman world, it was common for some of their heroes, usually saviors and healers to be called "sons of God." Therefore, Mark's early readers would have identified with this use of *the Son of God.*

2-3: *As it is written in the prophet Isaiah,* the messenger would prepare the people for the day of God's coming (Mal 3.1). Mark used a common trait and slightly changed the quoted text, "See, I am sending my messenger to prepare the way before me" (Mal 3.1), was changed to *"see, I am sending my messenger ahead of you"* so the prophecy referred to the Messiah. Then it was combined with the message from Isaiah, "A voice cries out in the wilderness 'prepare the way of the LORD, make straight in the desert a highway for our God'" (Isa 40.3). *Prepare the way of the LORD* was regarding the preparations for God to lead those in exile back home on a specially prepared straight highway. **4:** If Mark knew of the birth and infant traditions, he expressed no interest in them; instead, he began with the ministry of John the Baptist who appeared *in the wilderness* preaching *a baptism of repentance.* Some scholars hold that verses two and three are an insertion and connect verse four to one. John the Baptist was an important religious figure in his own right, with disciples that maintained their separate identity for a long time after his death. John called people to baptism with water, symbolizing recognition and confession of sin with acceptance of God's will. When a non-Jew became a Jew three things were required, the first was circumcision, as that was the mark of the covenant people. The second was to make a sacrifice for his sins, as only blood could atone for sin. The third was to be baptized, that symbolized the cleansing from the pollution of the past life. Baptism was not performed by

30

sprinkling, rather where the entire body was bathed. Then John, in *proclaiming a baptism of repentance* was asking the Jewish people to submit themselves to something that was only required of non-Jews. *For the forgiveness of sins* was possibly introduced into the text because of the early Christian view of baptism. **5-6:** *The whole Judean countryside and all the people of Jerusalem* as people from both the rural areas of Judah and the city of *Jerusalem* were *baptized by him,* or in his presence, or at his direction. Jewish baptisms and probably the earliest Christian baptisms were self-administered. *Gospel according to the Ebionites* (in *Epiphanius, Against Heresies,* 30.13.4), "John was baptizing; and Pharisees went out to him and were baptized, and all Jerusalem. Now John wore a garment of camel's hair, and a leather girdle around his waist; his food was wild honey, tasting like manna, like a cake in olive oil." **7-8:** The Talmud proclaimed that a disciple would perform every service for his master that a slave might do for him except to *stoop down and untie the thong of his sandals.* John did not consider himself *worthy* to do this for the one *who is more powerful.* Baptism *with the Holy Spirit* would draw people into a spiritual communion with God (Acts 2.17-21; Joel 2.28-29). The Q form has "he will baptize you with fire." Mark interpreted fire to be *Holy Spirit* that was followed by Luke in Acts, but Matthew and Luke used "Holy Spirit and fire" (Mt 3.11; Lk 3.16). The previous verses appeared to be the introduction to Jesus' public ministry. John's ministry was viewed as only preparing for the coming of Jesus Christ, with no effort made by Mark to present him as an historical figure, because Mark's emphasis was upon *"Jesus Christ, the Son of God."*

Jesus' baptism, 1.9-11

9-11: *In those days,* indicated that *John the Baptist* appeared while Jesus was living at Nazareth (Mt 2.23). Matthew stated that Jesus' purpose for leaving Galilee was to be baptized by John (Mt 3.13). *The heavens torn apart* may be a better translation than "opened" used by Matthew (Mt 3.16) and Luke (Lk 3.21) where the words of the heavenly voice are addressed directly to Jesus (cf Mk 15.38 where the curtain in the temple was torn in two, from the top to the bottom). *The dove* was a symbol of innocence, or moral purity, and the power of God. *A voice came from heaven* that combined Ps 2.7, an ancient hymn used for a royal accession or coronation, with Isaiah chapter 42, a part of the servant song of Deutero-Isaiah, "Here is my servant, whom I uphold, my chosen in whom my soul delights; he will bring forth justice to the nations" (Isa 42.1). For Mark, as for the early Gentile church, Jesus' divine Sonship was unique and wholly supernatural. *Gospel according to the Ebionites* (in Jerome, *Against Pelagius,* 3.2), "The mother of the Lord and his brothers said to him, 'John the Baptist baptizes for the forgiveness of sins; let us go and be baptized by him.' However, he said to them, 'In what way have I sinned that I should go and be baptized by him? Unless, perhaps, what I have just said is a sin of ignorance.'"

Jesus' temptation, 1.12-13

12-13: *Immediately,* a common word appeared forty-one times in Mark. Mark used a forceful expression, *the Spirit drove,* to describe how Jesus went into the wilderness. Matthew and Luke used "led by the Spirit" *in the wilderness* to indicate that Jesus had some choice in the matter. *Forty days in the wilderness* was in reference to the forty years that Israel was in the wilderness (Ex 24.18; 34.28). Mark and Luke had the temptations during the *forty days,* while Matthew placed the temptations after fasting *forty days* and nights. Unlike Matthew and Luke, Mark did not identify the temptations, but he added that Jesus *was with the wild beasts* and that *the angels waited on him.*

Beginnings of Jesus' activity in Galilee, 1.14-39

14: According to Mark, Jesus proclaimed *the good news of God* only after *John was arrested.* **15:** *The time is fulfilled* meant the time had come (cf Dan 7.22; Gal 4.4), *and the kingdom of God has* *come near,* or had begun to arrive. The question was when would it be completely established? While Mark placed an emphasis on the future fulfillment, his gospel was a record of the acts God had already accomplished (Lk 10.18; 11.20; 17.21). *Repent,* return to God's way, and *believe the good news,* accept the message, Mark illustrated by Jesus healing the ill, casting out the demons, and associating with sinners (Mt 4.17). Jesus' message differed from that of John the Baptist in there was no judgment.

16: *Passed along* meant walked by. The fishing *net* was a circular net used for casting. The net had stone weights around the circumference with a draw rope that could close it around the catch. *Sea of Galilee* was really a lake and was known as Sea of Tiberias and the Lake of Gennesaret. It was 12.5 miles long by 7.5 miles wide. **17:** *Follow me* conveyed the Jewish tradition where disciples only followed a teacher by invitation. Responding to Jesus' call, *they left their nets,* business, source of livelihood, family, and went with Jesus, to learn his message and to assist any way they could. (Mt 4.20; Lk 5.1-11; Jn 1.25-42). **20:** *With the hired men,* that was paid workers, indicated that Zebedee was not poor, but it did not indicate that he was rich either.

21: The *synagogue* was a lay institution established during the exile when Jews gathered on the sabbath to hear the scripture read and to offer prayer. After the destruction of the temple (70 CE), its primary purpose was education. It remains unclear why or when the "Sabbath" in the OT becomes *sabbath* in the NT, other than to reduce its importance and to increase the meaning of "the Lord's Day" to celebrate the resurrection of Jesus. **22:** *One having authority...not as the scribes* meant because Jesus spoke as a prophet, with direct authority from God, and not by citing various spiritual authorities to support his teaching. **23:** Jesus *went down* from the highlands of Galilee (Nazareth was thirteen hundred feet above sea level), *to Capernaum,* a city six hundred eighty-six feet below sea level. (The Dead Sea was twelve hundred nighty-two feet below sea level.) Capernaum was an important toll station on the trade route from

Ptolemais to Damascus. Luke identified this synagogue was built by a centurion (*see* Centurion), an officer in the Roman army (Lk 7.5).

24-26: The gospels reflected a widespread dread of demons with a feeling of helplessness regarding their activity. Jesus was portrayed here and elsewhere as one who could deliver people from demonic oppression and from Satan himself (Mk 12.22; Lk 4.31-37; 7.33; 13.16). Jesus became widely known as a healer, particularly of what are described as mental and nervous diseases. **24:** *Have you come to destroy us?* In late Judaism freeing individuals from enslavement to Belial and the destruction of the evil spirits was a function of the Messiah. The *spirit,* or demon, was called *unclean,* because the effect of the condition was to separate people from the worship of God. *The Holy One of God* was a messianic title (Jn 6.69). **27:** *"What is this? A new teaching with authority!"* The emphasis was upon Jesus' *authority* and power to command the unclean spirits to be silent and come out, as the powers of evil were being vanquished. And the news about Jesus spread.

29-31: Paul confirmed that Simon (Cephas) was a married man (1 Cor 9.5). Jesus entered the house and she *was in bed with a fever,* and *they,* assumed to be Simon, Andrew, James, and John, *told him about her at once.* Jesus *took her by the hand and lifted her up. Then the fever left her, and she began to serve them,* something in contrast to the Jewish tradition where men wait on the tables of men (Acts 6.2).

32: The sabbath ended at sunset and once again burdens were carried out and the *sick or possessed* were brought to Jesus (see 1.21n). **33:** *The door* was to Peter's house. **34:** *He cured many* did not imply that Jesus' powers to heal were limited, but that many were brought to him and he healed them (cf 6.5). *Would not permit the demons to speak because they knew him,* but he did not want them to proclaim his divine identity until the appropriate time.

35-39: Jesus sought *a deserted place, and there he prayed.* Mark recorded three times (6.31; 14.32) when Jesus prayed, and it was always at night when he sought God's direction. *Everyone* meant the people of Capernaum were looking for Jesus to heal their sick, but he wished to *go on to the neighboring towns* to do what he *came out to do* to *proclaim the message.*

Ministry and controversy, chiefly in Galilee, 1.40-9.50

Mark inserted this story of the healing of the leper as an example of Jesus' activity throughout Galilee. (Cf *Egerton Papyrus* 2.), "A person with leprosy came up to Jesus and said, 'Master Jesus, journeying with leprous people and eating with them in the inn, I also became leprous. If, therefore, you will, I can be made clean.' Then the Lord answered, 'I will; be clean.' And immediately the leprosy departed; and the Lord said, 'Go and show yourself to the priests.'"

40-44: Leprosy was a term that covered a variety of ulcerous diseases, some of them curable. The leper was expected to separate himself and to cry, "Unclean, unclean" as a warning to others of his condition (Lev 13.45-46). It would have been unlawful for a leper to approach anyone, yet Matthew (Mt 8.1-4) and Mark recorded the leper came to Jesus *and knelt before him* while Luke (Lk 5.12-14) implied that Jesus might have been passing by the leper. *If you choose, you can make me clean.* The leper not only wanted to be healed but the freedom to rejoin the Jewish community, and only when a priest had pronounced him *"clean"* and he had made the prescribed offering could he be readmitted to society (Lev 14.1-32). Mark had Jesus being moved with pity as he touched him saying, *"I do choose. Be made clean."* In Mark's gospel, Jesus went from pity for the leper to *"sternly"* warning him not to tell anyone, but to show himself to the priest. In other translations the word *"sternly"* was translated "strictly" because *"sternly"* in the Greek meant being very angry with him. Luke corrected this difficult account as Jesus ordered the leper, while Matthew just told the healed leper to *say nothing to anyone,* but he was to *show* himself to the *priest* and make an offering as *Moses commanded* according to religious rite and legal custom (Lev 14.2-32). While Matthew and Luke did not continue the account, Mark had the leper, instead of going to the priest, leaving and telling others how Jesus healed him. **45:** Apparently Jesus feared that rumors of miracles would gather the curious and foster cries for help only in physical terms hindering his ability to proclaim the message.

Chapter 1 Study Guide

1. Why did Mark write his gospel?
2. Describe the first disciples called by Jesus and what did it mean, "I will make you fish for people?"
3. Why did Mark early in his gospel describe Jesus cleansing the man with an unclean spirit?
4. Why did Jesus want to leave Capernaum and go to neighboring towns?
5. Why did Jesus in an act of compassion heal the leper and then sternly warn him not to say anything to anyone, but to go and show himself to the priest and make an offering?

Chapter 2
Healing a paralytic, 2.1-12
(Mt 9.1-8; Lk 5.17-26)

Mark. [Q₂][When he returned to Capernaum after some days, it was reported that he was at home.] ² So many gathered around that there was no longer room for them, not even in front of the door; and he was speaking the word to them. ³Then some people[a] came, bringing to him a paralyzed man, carried by four of them. ⁴And when they could not bring him to Jesus because of the crowd, they removed the roof above him; and after having dug through it, they let down the mat on which the paralytic lay. ⁵When Jesus saw their faith, he said to the paralytic,

Jesus. "Son, your sins are forgiven."

_____
[a] Gk *they*

Mark. [6]Now some of the scribes were sitting there, questioning in their hearts,

Scribes. [7]"Why does this fellow speak in this way? It is blasphemy! Who can forgive sins but God alone?"

Mark. [8]At once Jesus perceived in his spirit that they were discussing these questions among themselves; and he said to them,

Jesus. "Why do you raise such questions in your hearts? [9]Which is easier, to say to the paralytic, 'Your sins are forgiven,' or to say, 'Stand up and take your mat and walk'? [10]But so that you may know that the Son of Man has authority on earth to forgive sins"

Mark. He said to the paralytic

Jesus. [11]"I say to you, stand up, take your mat and go to your home."

Mark. [12]And he stood up, and immediately took the mat and went out before all of them; so that they were all amazed and glorified God, saying,

Crowd. "We have never seen anything like this!"

The call of Lev, 2.13-17
(Mt 9.9-13; Lk 5.27-32)

Mark. [13]Jesus[b] went out again beside the sea; the whole crowd gathered around him, and he taught them. [14]As he was walking along, he saw Levi son of Alphaeus sitting at the tax booth, and he said to him,

Jesus. "Follow me."

Mark. And he got up and followed him.

---

[b] Gk *He*

37

[15] And as he sat at dinner[c] in Levi's[d] house, many tax collectors and sinners were also sitting[e] with Jesus and his disciples—for there were many who followed him. [16] When the scribes of[f] the Pharisees saw that he was eating with sinners and tax collectors, they said to his disciples,

Scribes. "Why does he eat[g] with tax collectors and sinners?"

Mark. [17] When Jesus heard this, he said to them,

Jesus. "Those who are well have no need of a physician, but those who are sick; I have come to call not the righteous but sinners."

Fasting, 2.18-22
(Mt 9.14-17; Lk 5.33-39)

Mark. [18] Now John's disciples and the Pharisees were fasting; and people[h] came and said to him,

People. "Why do John's disciples and the disciples of the Pharisees fast, but your disciples do not fast?"

Mark. [19] Jesus said to them,

Jesus. "The wedding guests cannot fast while the bridegroom is with them, can they? As long as they have the bridegroom with them, they cannot fast. [20] The days will come when the bridegroom is taken away from them, and then they will fast on that day.
[21] "No one sews a piece of unshrunk cloth on an old cloak; otherwise, the patch pulls away from it, the new from the old, and a worse tear is made. [22] And no one puts new wine into old wineskins;

---

[c] Gk *reclined*
[d] Gk *his*
[e] Gk *reclining*
[f] Other ancient authorities read *and*
[g] Other ancient authorities add *and drink*
[h] Gk *they*

otherwise, the wine will burst the skins, and the wine is lost, and so are the skins; but one puts new wine into fresh wineskins."[i]

Jesus and the sabbath laws, 2.23-3.6
(Mt 12.1-14; Lk 6.1-11)

Mark. [23]One sabbath he was going through the grainfields; and as they made their way his disciples began to pluck heads of grain. [24]The Pharisees said to him,

Pharisees. "Look, why are they doing what is not lawful on the sabbath?"

Mark. [25]And he said to them,

Jesus. "Have you never read what David did when he and his companions were hungry and in need of food? [26] He entered the house of God, when Abiathar was high priest, and ate the bread of the Presence, which it is not lawful for any but the priests to eat, and he gave some to his companions."

Mark. [27] Then he said to them,

Jesus. "The sabbath was made for humankind, and not humankind for the sabbath; [28] so the Son of Man is lord even of the sabbath."

Chapter 2 Notes
Healing a paralytic, 2.1-12

Mark included in 2.1-3.6 a series of conflicts and controversies to reveal the growing opposition to Jesus by the scribes and Pharisees. Mark may have inserted the opening conflict (vss. 5b-10) into the story, because Jesus addressed the paralytic twice, once in v 5 and then again in v 10. The story reads well enough without those verses

---

[i] Other ancient authorities lack *but one puts new wine into fresh wineskins*

and resembles a form present in other healing narratives. However, for Mark the good news was that God through Jesus took the first step of healing humanity without waiting for an expression of repentance, an act that ignited controversy.

1: Jesus returned to his hometown, Capernaum. Mark (Mk 2.1-12) and Luke (Lk 5.17-26) have Jesus teaching at home rather than in the synagogue in *Capernaum,* while Matthew implied that the paralyzed man was brought to Jesus as he arrived in the land (Mt 9.1-8). **2:** *The word* was everything he had to say to people about God's purposes. **4:** The house was a one story, maybe, a one-room house. The crowd spilled outside preventing access through the door. The *roof* would be a flat thatch of straw or branches, coated with clay and reached by an outside staircase. The *mat* would be more like a rug or stretcher. **5:** There was no reason to deny that the paralytic had *faith,* but Mark stressed the *faith* of his helpers. When Jesus said, *"Your sins are forgiven,"* he claimed a divine right, as did the apostles and the church after him. The church taught that baptism marked the annulment of past sins and the beginning of a new life (Mt 6.9-15; 2 Cor 2.5-11). **7:** This differed from the OT and rabbinical tradition where it was a divine prerogative to proclaim forgiveness of sins (Ex 34.6-7; Isa 43.25-26; 44.22). The difference here was that Jesus pronounced the forgiveness of a person's sin independent of the prescribed sin offering or the Day of Atonement offering, or any evidence of the sinner's repentance (Lev 4-7; 16). No one *can forgive sins* except *God,* not even the Messiah, according to the rabbis. **8:** With spiritual insight, he knew *what they were discussing among themselves.* Later rabbinic teaching held that blasphemy, or wrong speech, concerning God was punishable by death (*Mishnah Sanhedrin,* 7.5). **9:** It would have been *easier* to say, *"Your sins are forgiven"* than *"stand up and take your mat and walk,"* because no one but God could tell if the pronouncement was correct. **10:** *Son of Man* was a title that only occurred in the gospels from the lips of Jesus and seemed to his listeners to carry either of two meanings: (a) that Jesus called himself a typical human being under the common meaning of *son of* someone such as Joseph; or (b) that Jesus (contrary to the humble conditions of his daily life) linked himself to the prophesied figure of Daniel (Dan 7.13-14), who was popularly regarded as the coming Messiah. However, each meaning, the Son of Man or Messiah, by itself, and both together, could have appealed to Jesus. It was also characteristic of him to speak in such a way as to oblige his hearers to determine their own personal attitudes toward him as part of understanding his words. By doing the harder task, Jesus proved he had *authority on earth to forgive sins.* **11-12:** The cure was verified by the paralytic's response, *he stood up, and immediately took up his mat and went out.* The people were *amazed and glorified God.*

The call of Levi, 2.13-17

13: *The sea* was of Galilee. **14:** A *tax collector,* better described as an enforcer, had the right to collect a Roman tax. Mark identified *Levi* as *"the son of Alphaeus."* All of the Synoptic Gospels included James *"the son of Alphaeus"* in the list of the disciples, but there was no Levi. Matthew had a similar story about a tax collector by the name of Matthew, who was included as a member of the inner circle. The importance was not the name, but that Jesus sought to draw in (call) the outcasts that the Pharisees excluded from society. **15:** *Levi* held *a dinner* for *Jesus and his disciples* and invited a large group of his *tax collector* friends and other *sinners.* It remained unclear if the *scribes of the Pharisees* were part of the dinner, but they were probably outside *complaining to his disciples.* The rabbis concluded that sharing a meal with those who ignored the law was among those "things that shame a pupil of the scribes." For Luke the issue may have been Judaism's charge that the Gentiles and other riffraff were being welcomed into the membership of the early Christian church. **16:** *Sinners* here meant the Jewish people who did not observe the dietary and others laws. The hostilities between the tax collectors and the Pharisees are explained in a remark of *R. Akiba* (132 CE), "When I was a tax collector I used to say, 'If I could get hold of one of the scholars I would bite him like an ass.' 'You mean, like a dog,' said his disciples. 'No,' said Akiba, 'an ass's bite breaks bones.'" Mark used *disciples* here, but he usually referred to them as the Twelve to distinguish them from the many that followed Jesus. **17:** Jesus sought to draw in (call) the outcasts that the Pharisees excluded from society, this superseded defilement and the fear of it (Prov 14.21).

Fasting, 2.18-22

18: *John's* that was the Baptist's *disciples. Fasting* was only required on the Day of Atonement. Special fasts were proclaimed during times of emergencies, such as a drought. The disciples of John and the Pharisees as a special act of devotion fasted on Mondays and Thursdays. Cf *Didache,* 8:1, "Do not fast with the hypocrites, for they fast on the second and fifth days of the week (i.e., Mondays and Thursdays); but you should fast on the fourth day and on the day of Preparation (i.e., Wednesdays and Fridays)." **19-20:** Some wondered why Jesus' disciples did not follow the example of *John's disciples and the disciples of the Pharisees.* The implication was that Jesus came as a *bridegroom* for his followers (the bride). Fasting was inappropriate at a wedding and with the joyous association with himself. John the Baptist refused to share in his disciples' concern and affirmed he was only the friend of the bridegroom, leading Israel, the bride, to Jesus, the bridegroom (Jn 3.27-29). Mark for the first time revealed the shadow of the cross by his words *when the bridegroom is taken from them.* Cf *Gospel of Thomas,* Logion 27 and 104b, [27] Jesus said, "If you do not fast from the world you will not find the kingdom; if you do not keep the sabbath as sabbath you will not see the Father." [104] "When the bridegroom comes out of the bridal chamber, then let them fast and let them pray."

21: Mark and Matthew stated that a patch of *unshrunk cloth* would shrink after it had been sewed on an *old cloak,* leaving a tear worse than before (Mt 9.16). Luke (Lk 5.36) placed a different emphasis stating that *no one tears a piece from a new garment* that meant ruining a new garment to patch *an old* one since the piece *from the new will not match the old. New wine* was unfermented wine. *Old wineskins* were hard and dry and *would burst* when the fermentation occurred. These parables taught that you should not mix the new with the old, but they did not pass judgment on the merits of the one to the other. In their application they point out that the new Christian message and the old forms of Judaism were incompatible, and that the new gospel had nothing to do with the old ritual of fasting.

Jesus and the sabbath laws, 2.23-3.6

24: Rabbinical tradition added to the OT prohibition of sabbath labor thirty-nine "major occupations" including harvesting and threshing (*Mishnah Sabbath,* 7:2). To pluck heads of grain in a neighbor's field was not considered stealing (Deut 23.25), but to do it on the sabbath was *"harvesting"* and therefore breaking the law. **25:** Jesus defended the disciples' actions by referring to David's action *when he was hungry* (1 Sam 21.1-6). Human needs can override the letter of the law. Matthew and Luke omitted Mark's mistaken reference to Abiathar (instead of Ahimelech) as high priest. **26:** *The bread of the Presence* was twelve cakes placed each sabbath on a "table of pure gold" in the sanctuary and only eaten by priests (Lev 24.5-9). **27:** Since no penalty was exacted from those who set aside provisions of the law for the sake of some human need or more significant service to God, Jesus' disciples ate because of their need and served him who was greater than the institutions of the law (*see* vs 41-42). **28:** No doubt, the early church found this argument useful in its controversy with the Jewish officials over the celebration of the Christian Sunday as all three of the synoptic writers declared *the Son of Man is lord of the Sabbath* (Mt 12.8; Lk 6.5). Jesus claimed, by his mission as the Messiah, authority over another's obedience to God (11.27; Jn 5.1-18). Cf *Gospel of Thomas*, Logion 27b, Jesus said, "If you do not keep the sabbath as sabbath you will not see the Father."

Chapter 2 Study Guide

1. Was God the only one that could forgive sins?
2. Why did the gospel writers include the call of Levi and Jesus and the disciples eating with tax collectors and sinners?
3. What is your reaction to "those who are well have no need of a physician"?
4. Explain the example of the bridegroom as used by the gospel writers.
5. Can the old endure the new in patterns of religion and culture?

Chapter 3

Mark. Again he entered the synagogue, and a man was there who had a withered hand. ² They watched him to see whether he would cure him on the sabbath, so that they might accuse him. ³ And he said to the man who had the withered hand,

Jesus. "Come forward."

Mark. ⁴ Then he said to them,

Jesus. "Is it lawful to do good or to do harm on the sabbath, to save life or to kill?"

Mark. But they were silent. ⁵ He looked around at them with anger; he was grieved at their hardness of heart and said to the man,

Jesus. "Stretch out your hand."

Mark. He stretched it out, and his hand was restored. ⁶ The Pharisees went out and immediately conspired with the Herodians against him, how to destroy him.

Work of healing, 3.7-12
(Mt 4.24-25; 12.15-21; Lk 6.17-19)

Mark. [7]Jesus departed with his disciples to the sea, and a great multitude from Galilee followed him; [8]hearing all that he was doing, they came to him in great numbers from Judea, Jerusalem, Idumea, beyond the Jordan, and the region around Tyre and Sidon. [9]He told his disciples to have a boat ready for him because of the crowd, so that they would not crush him; [10]for he had cured many, so that all who had diseases pressed upon him to touch him. [11]Whenever the unclean spirits saw him, they fell down before him and shouted,

Demons. "You are the Son of God!"

Mark. [12]But he sternly ordered them not to make him known.

The Twelve chosen, 3.13-19a
(Mt 10.1-4; Lk 6.12-16)

Mark. [13]He went up the mountain and called to him those whom he wanted, and they came to him. [14]And he appointed twelve, whom he also named apostles,[a] to be with him, and to be sent out to proclaim the message, [15]and to have authority to cast out demons. [16]So he appointed the twelve:[b] Simon (to whom he gave the name Peter); [17]James son of Zebedee and John the brother of James (to whom he gave the name Boanerges, that is, Sons of Thunder); [18]and Andrew, and Philip, and Bartholomew, and Matthew, and Thomas, and James son of Alphaeus, and Thaddaeus, and Simon the Cananaean, [19]and Judas Iscariot, who betrayed him.

---

[a] Other ancient authorities lack *whom he also named apostles*
[b] Other ancient authorities lack *So he appointed the twelve*

Questions about Jesus' power, 3.19b-35
(Mt 12.22-37; Lk 11.14-23; 12.10; 6.43-45)

Mark. Then he went home; [20] and the crowd came together again, so that they could not even eat. [21] When his family heard it, they went out to restrain him, for people were saying,

People. "He has gone out of his mind."

Mark. [Q₂][[22] And the scribes who came down from Jerusalem said,

Scribes. "He has Beelzebul, and by the ruler of the demons he casts out demons."

Mark. [23]And he called them to him, and spoke to them in parables,

Jesus. "How can Satan cast out Satan? [24] If a kingdom is divided against itself, that kingdom cannot stand. [25] And if a house is divided against itself, that house will not be able to stand. [26] And if Satan has risen up against himself and is divided, he cannot stand, but his end has come. [27]But no one can enter a strong man's house and plunder his property without first tying up the strong man; then indeed the house can be plundered.]

[Q₂][[28] "Truly I tell you, people will be forgiven for their sins and whatever blasphemies they utter; [29] but whoever blasphemes against the Holy Spirit can never have forgiveness, but is guilty of an eternal sin"]

Mark. [30] for they had said,

Scribes. "He has an unclean spirit."

Mark. [31] Then his mother and his brothers came; and standing outside, they sent to him and called him. [32]A crowd was sitting around him; and they said to him,

Crowd. "Your mother and your brothers and sisters[c] are outside, asking for you."

Mark. [33]And he replied,

Jesus. "Who are my mother and my brothers?"

Mark. [34] And looking at those who sat around him, he said,

Jesus. "Here are my mother and my brothers! **[Q₁][**[35] Whoever does the will of God**]** is my brother and sister and mother."

Chapter 3 Notes

In the first sabbath controversy the disciples were attacked for not observing it (2.24), and now the accusation was directed to Jesus. **1:** *Again* meant another example was given. Nothing was said about the man except that he *had a withered hand.* Luke added that it was his *right hand.* According to Jerome, *Gospel according to the Hebrews*, the man was described as a mason, who depended on his hands, and who pleaded for Jesus to heal him with the following words: "I was a mason, earning a living with my hands; I beg you, Jesus, restore my health to me, so that I need not beg for my food in shame." **2:** *They watched him,* the Pharisees were eager *to see if he would cure him on the sabbath,* not to rejoice in the wholeness of the man, but *so they might accuse him.* **3-4:** Jesus acted by the principle previously stated (Mk 2.27) and equated acts to meet human need with acts *lawful ... on the sabbath.* For Jesus to heal was to save a life and to neglect the opportunity for wholeness, merely because it was the sabbath, was *to kill* (Lk 14.3). **5:** *With anger, he was grieved at their hardness of heart* reflected the feelings that Jesus had towards the Pharisees inhumanity, bigotry and fanaticism. Jesus told the man to *stretch out* his *hand, and his hand was restored.* **6:** *Herodians* were apparently

---

c Other ancient authorities lack *and sisters*

a group supporting the royal family. Josephus (*Jewish Antiquities,* 14.15.10) recorded the Herodians were interested in putting down any movement, like that of John the Baptist, that endangered the current political order. The Pharisees sought allies wherever they might be found (12.13) as they *conspired,* not to heal on the sabbath, but *how to destroy* Jesus.

Work of healing, 3.7-12

7-8: Motivated by the desires of his enemies and because his fame had spread, *Jesus* and *his disciples* withdrew *to the sea.* However, *a great multitude,* including people from *Judea, Jerusalem, Idumea, and beyond the Jordan, and the region of Tyre and Sidon followed.* These were all parts of Palestine inhabited by Jews. The absence of Samaria in the list has been noted. The people of Idumea were forced to become Jewish by John Hyrcanus, and they are omitted by some ancient authorities. **9:** The disciples' order to *have a boat ready for him,* where he could teach, was not included in Matthew or Luke. **10:** The popular belief was that *all who had diseases* would be healed, if they could *touch him* (Mk 6.56; Mt 4.24; 14.36). **11:** Mark was sure that the *unclean spirits* recognized Jesus, *they fell down before him and shouted, "You are the Son of God."* **12:** *Sternly* in the Greek translated to "very angrily" (1.43 n).

The Twelve chosen, 3.13-19a

Jesus invited the Twelve to live intimately with him, adopting his way of life and his message. Spiritual strength came through the community he established (see 6.7-13n). **13-16:** The call and training of the Twelve occupied an important place for each of the gospel writers, yet each used it for their own purpose. Matthew devoted a major section to the training of the disciples (Mt 8.1-11.1) and placed it immediately following the Sermon on the Mount intended for all his followers. Luke had the Twelve chosen just before his Sermon on the Plain (6.12-16), but their training continued after the resurrection

(Lk 24.25-53; Acts 1.1-11). John placed the call of the Twelve early in his gospel (Jn 1.35-51), because his entire book was an education of the disciples, with the mission and person of Christ revealed in the upper room, on the Mount of Olives (Jn 13-17; 20.19-29), with a final appearance at the Sea of Galilee (21.15-22). Mark placed the choice of the Twelve at this point while their training continued in stages, with a climax in chapter 13, and then they were told to go to Galilee to see him (16.7). Just as John the Baptist (1.2) and Jesus (9.37; 12.2-6) were sent by God, so Jesus appointed the Twelve to continue the work he had begun. **14:** Mark often referred to the Twelve as "disciples" (2.15-16, 18, 23; 4.34; 6.35, etc), but he did not always distinguish them from a larger group of followers unless he called them the Twelve (6.7; 9.35; 10.32; 11.11; 14.10, 17, 20, 43). The term *apostles* could include the Twelve, but it seemed in reference to anyone, including Paul, who had a commission to proclaim the gospel (Rom 1.1, 16.7; 1 Cor 9.5; Gal 1.1, 19; Acts 14.14). When Matthew spoke of the "twelve disciples" (Mt 10.1), it may have been regarding special students of a rabbi or teacher. **16-18:** Simon was usually listed first among the disciples. His name in Greek was Peter and in Aramaic translated to *"rock"* (Gal 1.18; 1 Cor 1.12; Jn 1.42). **3:** The "bar" in *Bartholomew* usually meant "son of" but the rest of the name was uncertain. *Thomas* was often identified as "the twin" and may be from the Aramaic word for twin (Jn 11.16; 20.24). Matthew was identified as the tax collector (9.9). *James* was identified as the *son of Alphaeus* to distinguish him from James the son of Zebedee (Mk 2.14). *Thaddaeus,* was in some manuscripts called "Lebbaeus" which may indicate that the early church was not sure about his identity. *Simeon the Cananaean* identified Simon as a zealot that came from the Aramaic word *Cananaean* (Lk 6.15; Acts 1.13)**.** *Judas* was always listed last and his betrayal of Jesus was noted. *Iscariot* may come from the Aramaic word meaning "the false" or from a place in Judea, and if so, he would have been the only non-Galilean among the disciples (Lk 6.15; Acts 1.13).

Questions about Jesus' power, 3.19b-35

22: The charge that an individual was connected with the forces of evil was a dangerous one in a superstitious age. Mark had this charge made by the *"scribes"* and in Matthew it was by "the Pharisees" (Mt 12.24). Luke had "some in the crowd" (Lk 11.15) that probably represented Q. *Beelzebul* was derived from the Hebrew text of 2 Kings (2 Kings 1.2-3), where Baalzebub (lord of flies) was a mocking distortion of Baalzebul (lord of the temple), the name of the god of Ekron. In Aramaic Beelzebul was interpreted *"lord of dung."* None have been found in Jewish literature as a name for Satan. **23-24:** *How can Satan cast out Satan* as it would be against his interest? Mark used the Hebrew name for the tempter (Mk 1.13). Matthew and Luke (Mt 12.27-28; Lk 11.19-20) have the power of exorcising demons not limited to Jesus and his followers, but also included the Pharisees. The point was if Jesus casted out demons by Beelzebul, where did the Pharisees' power to do the same come from? **27:** How can *a strong man's house be entered* unless someone who was stronger tied *up the strong man?* If the man became blind and a mute by Beelzebul that in being healed by the Spirit of God in Jesus than Jesus was stronger than Beelzebul.

28-29: *Blasphemy against the Spirit,* the unforgivable sin, was the utter rebellion against God that denied him as the doer of his own acts (Mt 12.31-32; Lk 12.10).

31-35: Matthew (Mt 12.46-50) and Luke (Lk 8.19-21) have similar sayings where bonds of the spirit bind the family of God. According to Mark's account, Jesus' family was disturbed by the rumor he was a lunatic and had come to take him home. In Luke's version, all of this had disappeared and those who heard the word of God and do it were identified as members of the family. Matthew had the membership based upon whoever did the will of my Father in heaven. There was no reason to believe that the *brothers* here were not his brothers in the usual sense of the word.

Chapter 3 Study Guide

1. How do you explain Jesus healing on the sabbath?
2. Why did Jesus choose and train the twelve disciples?
3. Why did Mark have Jesus' family wanting to restrain him?
4. Explain the example of the strong man.
5. What are the qualifications for membership into Jesus' family?

Chapter 4
Teaching in parables, 4.1-34
(Mt ch 13; Lk 8.4-18, 13.18-21)

Mark. Again he began to teach beside the sea. Such a very large crowd gathered around him that he got into a boat on the sea and sat there, while the whole crowd was beside the sea on the land. ² He began to teach them many things in parables, and in his teaching he said to them:

Jesus. ³ "Listen! A sower went out to sow. ⁴ And as he sowed, some seed fell on the path, and the birds came and ate it up. ⁵ Other seed fell on rocky ground, where it did not have much soil, and it sprang up quickly, since it had no depth of soil. ⁶And when the sun rose, it was scorched; and since it had no root, it withered away. ⁷ Other seed fell among thorns, and the thorns grew up and choked it, and it yielded no grain. ⁸ Other seed fell into good soil and brought forth grain, growing up and increasing and yielding thirty and sixty and a hundredfold."

Mark. ⁹And he said,

Jesus. "Let anyone with ears to hear listen!"

Mark. ¹⁰When he was alone, those who were around him along with the twelve asked him about the parables. ¹¹ And he said to them,

Jesus. "To you has been given the secret[a] of the kingdom of God, but for those outside, everything comes in parables; [12] in order that

Lord. (I)('they may indeed look, but not perceive, and may indeed listen, but not understand; so that they may not turn again and be forgiven.'" [b])

Mark. [13]And he said to them,

Jesus. "Do you not understand this parable? Then how will you understand all the parables? [14]The sower sows the word. [15]These are the ones on the path where the word is sown: when they hear, Satan immediately comes and takes away the word that is sown in them. [16]And these are the ones sown on rocky ground: when they hear the word, they immediately receive it with joy. [17]But they have no root, and endure only for a while; then, when trouble or persecution arises on account of the word, immediately they fall away.[c] [18] And others are those sown among the thorns: these are the ones who hear the word, [19] but the cares of the world, and the lure of wealth, and the desire for other things come in and choke the word, and it yields nothing. [20] And these are the ones sown on the good soil: they hear the word and accept it and bear fruit, thirty and sixty and a hundredfold."

Mark. [21]He said to them,

Jesus. [Q₂]["Is a lamp brought in to be put under the bushel basket, or under the bed, and not on the lampstand?] [Q₁][[22] For there is nothing hidden, except to be disclosed; nor is anything secret, except to come to light.] [23] Let anyone with ears to hear listen!"

Mark. [24]And he said to them,

---

[a] Or *mystery*
[b] Isa 6.9-10
[c] Or *stumble*

Jesus. [Q₁]["Pay attention to what you hear; the measure you give will be the measure you get, and still more will be given you.] [Q₂][²⁵ For to those who have, more will be given; and from those who have nothing, even what they have will be taken away."]

The seed growing secretly, 4.26-29
(Mt 13.24-30)

Mark. ²⁶He also said,

Jesus. "The kingdom of God is as if someone would scatter seed on the ground, ²⁷ and would sleep and rise night and day, and the seed would sprout and grow, he does not know how. ²⁸ The earth produces of itself, first the stalk, then the head, then the full grain in the head. ²⁹ But when the grain is ripe, at once he goes in with his sickle, because the harvest has come."

The mustard seed, 4.30-34
(Mt 13.31-32; Lk 13.18-19)

Mark. ³⁰He also said,

Jesus. [Q₁]["With what can we compare the kingdom of God, or what parable will we use for it? ³¹ It is like a mustard seed, which, when sown upon the ground, is the smallest of all the seeds on earth; ³² yet when it is sown it grows up and becomes the greatest of all shrubs, and puts forth large branches, so that the birds of the air can make nests in its shade."]

Mark. ³³ With many such parables he spoke the word to them, as they were able to hear it; ³⁴ he did not speak to them except in parables, but he explained everything in private to his disciples.

Wind and sea calmed, 4.35-41
(Mt 8.18, 23-27; Lk 8.22-25)

Mark. [35]On that day, when evening had come, he said to them,

Jesus. "Let us go across to the other side."

Mark. [36]And leaving the crowd behind, they took him with them in the boat, just as he was. Other boats were with him. [37] A great windstorm arose, and the waves beat into the boat, so that the boat was already being swamped. [38] But he was in the stern, asleep on the cushion; and they woke him up and said to him,

Disciples. "Teacher, do you not care that we are perishing?"

Mark. [39]He woke up and rebuked the wind, and said to the sea,

Jesus. "Peace! Be still!"

Mark. Then the wind ceased, and there was a dead calm. [40] He said to them,

Jesus. "Why are you afraid? Have you still no faith?"

Mark. [41]And they were filled with great awe and said to one another,

Disciples. "Who then is this, that even the wind and the sea obey him?"

Chapter 4 Notes
Teaching in parables, 4.1-34

In this chapter Mark presented Jesus teaching about the kingdom of God to the crowd in a public manner and the Twelve he had chosen (3.13-19) privately by parables. Jesus had proclaimed this message before in Galilee (1.14-15) and had emphasized the authorative nature of his words (1.21-22), and now for the second time (2.13) he proclaimed it by the sea. *Parables* are stories describing situations in everyday life, which, as Jesus used them, conveyed a spiritual meaning (*see* Jesus as Teacher). The teaching of each parable related to a single point, and apart from this the details may, or may not, have a particular meaning. Jesus used this method of teaching because: (*a*) it gave vivid, memorable expression to his teachings; (*b*) it led those who heard to reflect on his words and bear responsibility for their decision to accept or oppose his claim; (*c*) it probably reduced grounds for contention by hostile listeners; (*d*) so people could retell it.

Yet, two issues confronted all of the gospel writers beginning with Mark that dealt with the meaning of the parable. It is possible that many of the parables had lost their original meaning because the historical situation had changed for the hearers. Mark placed the parable of the sower immediately following the selection of the Twelve (3.13-19), next were questions about his power (3.19-30) and who was considered to be part of his family. Surrounded by the crowd and his disciples, Jesus said, "Whoever does the will of God is my brother and sister and mother" with no indication that Jesus' family was restricted to the Twelve (3.31-35).

However, the second issue confronting the gospel writers was the continued rejection of Jesus by the Jewish people even when he spoke to them with the authority of God (3.19-30). Therefore, Mark, and later Matthew and Luke, much like Paul (Rom 9-11) must have reasoned that God either willed, or limited the crowd's understanding of the parables presented by Jesus, but not that of the chosen ones. This is presented in the gospels as now the reason for the use of the parables. This became the opinion of an early church writer, Clement of Alexandria, *Miscellanies,* V.10:63, 7, "My secret is for me and the offspring of my house."

1: *Again he began to teach* implied that these three parables may have been used to encourage the Twelve as they proclaimed the message of the kingdom. They were to not worry about the seed that was lost, but focus on what succeeded, and once the seed was sown the result was in God's hands, and lastly to observe the results of even the smallest of seeds, the mustard seed (4.30-34). Mark had Jesus beginning his teaching *beside the sea* and being forced by *a very large crowd* to put out in a boat and teach offshore. **3:** *Listen* suggested the urgency of the message, "Hear, O Israel" (Deut 6.4), and for the hearer to exercise understanding. *Gospel of Thomas,* 82.3-13 began the parable with, "Whoever has ears to hear, let him hear" instead of ending it with those words (v 9). **4-9:** Mark's seed that *"fell on the path"* was expanded by Luke, "and was trampled on," before the birds ate them. Matthew and Mark have other *"seeds fall on rocky ground"* that does not have much soil, but Luke has the seed fall on "rock" where it 'withers" because of lack of moisture. All of the Synoptic Gospel writers have the seed that *fell among* the *thorns* being *choked* after they grew up. It was the seed that fell on the *good soil* that yielded *"thirty", "sixty",* and *"a hundredfold"* per Matthew and Mark while Luke had *"a hundredfold."*

10: Matthew (Mk 13.10) assumed the disciples asked Jesus why he spoke to them in parables when the crowd was absent, but Mark still had them present. In Mark and Luke (Lk 8.9), the disciples asked Jesus to interpret the parable of the sower to them. However, before Jesus answered the question, he told the disciples that they were different because to them has been given the secret of the kingdom of God ("heaven" in Matthew). Clement of Alexandria, *Miscellanies,* V.10.63,7, "Not grudgingly did the Lord declare in a certain gospel, 'My secret is for me and the offspring of my house.'" Jesus' response to the disciples was difficult to understand since the subject of the parables was the kingdom. Matthew (Mt 13.12) added that those who have been given the ability to understand would be given even greater insights, while those who have nothing, even that would be taken away. *Gospel of Thomas,* Logion 41, *"Jesus said,* 'all who have in their hand, to them shall be given; and all who do not have, from them shall be taken away, even the little they have.'" **12:** Jesus used the quote from Isaiah (Isa 6.9-10) to explain why he spoke to the crowds in parables. In Isaiah, the LORD (*see* LORD) told the prophet that the stubborn people would not heed his message that must be presented by the prophet. Matthew used this to predict that the Jewish people would not understand or hear the message that Jesus taught. All of the Synoptic Gospel writers affirm that they heard, but did not comprehend the truth. Matthew said it was because their hearts have grown dull, their ears were plugged and their eyes were shut. Mark seemed to say that Jesus taught in parables, not to make the truth about the kingdom known, but to conceal the truth from the masses or they would repent or change their attitudes and be forgiven. Matthew's position was softer and conveyed that the people would repent and be healed. However, Jesus used the parables to illustrate, to clarify, to reveal the truth and to allow the hearer to reflect upon the truth and to make a decision about the kingdom.

13-20: It was not clear if these words were those of Jesus or those of someone in the early church. It was not the custom for Jesus to explain his parables in allegorical detail. The interpretation seemed to refer to times after the resurrection when the Christian message was proclaimed to those who were in danger of losing their zeal for the faith. **14:** The sower sowed the message, which can be taken to be the message about Christ. Now the parable took on a description of four differing types of hearers. The first was the unresponsive hearer where the word received no understanding. **15:** The Evil One, Satan or Devil was usually pictured as a serpent (Rev 12.9) or a dragon (Rev 13.3), but not usually as a bird. The intent here is that he blocked the acceptance of the gospel and took away the unresponsive hearer's opportunity to receive it. **16-17:** The second hearer was a shallow hearer, one that lacked deep roots. He understood that the message was important, but his faith and commitment lacked depth and persistence. **18-19:** The third hearer let concern for material matters crowd out his loyalty to God. His life was cluttered up with material concerns and worries as he tried to serve God and the world. **20:** The fourth hearer heard the word, accepted it and God's will on his life and received the joy of living a life of obedience to God. There appeared to be no blame or punishment attached to the lesser harvests, only that good soil, properly cultivated, will yield a richer harvest.

21: After lighting *a lamp,* each of the Synoptic Gospel writers placed it *on a lampstand* instead of hiding it *under a bushel basket* (a pan or container holding about eight quarts used by Matthew), or *"under the bed"* (as here in Mark), or "under a jar" (as in Luke). Instead, the light was put *on the lampstand* where Matthew said *it gives light to all in the house,* while Mark did not indicate the location of the lampstand. Luke placed the *lampstand* in the vestibule of a Greco-Roman dwelling so that "those who enter may see the light" (Mk 4.21; Lk 8.16, 11.33). **24:** *Pay attention to what you hear.* God would give more truth to those who have listened to what he had already said, *for to those who have, more will be given.*

The seed growing secretly, 4.26-29

26-28: This parable expressed the theme of patience. Once a seed was sown, do not worry because the result was in God's hands. A companion theme was developed in the parable of the mustard seed and may have been the thoughts behind Matthew's parable of the weeds in the wheat (Mt 13.24-30). It was the *earth* not the *sower* or the *seed* that produced *the harvest.* **29:** This verse was a quote from Joel (Joel 3.13) which stressed waiting patiently for the *harvest.* Mark may have used this parable to address the issue about the apparent delay of the kingdom coming, as the result was put into place at the beginning.

The Mustard Seed, 4.30-34

30-31: Jews sowed *mustard seed in fields,* it was forbidden by the rabbis to sow it in a garden (*Mishnah Kilayim,* 3.2) and therefore Matthew (Mt 13.31-32) was preferred over Luke (Lk 13.19). Mustard was cultivated for its seed and as a vegetable. The *mustard seed* was the smallest seed, but it produced a large plant of ten feet in height. The parable stressed though the beginnings of God's kingdom were small, it would grow to its intended end, startlingly different in size from its beginning. **32:** *So that the birds of the air come and make* *nests in its branches* was a reference to Daniel (Dan 4.21) where Nebuchadnezzar's kingdom appeared in a vision as a great tree whose top reached to heaven, "under which animals of the fields lived, and in whose branches the bird of the air had nests." It was possible this verse was added by the early church. *Gospel of Thomas,* Logion 20, "The disciples said to Jesus, 'Tell us what the kingdom of heaven is like.' Jesus said to them, 'It is like a mustard seed, smaller than all seeds. But when it falls on the tilled ground, it produces a large branch and becomes a shelter for the birds of heaven.'"

Wind and sea calmed, 4.35-41

35-41: Nature miracles formed a small group in the gospels. Mark and Luke understood the incident of calming the sea as a display of his supernatural powers. Sudden *windstorms* were a common occurrence on the Sea of Galilee. *Faith* here meant trusting in the providence of God. Luke (Lk 8.22-25) followed a similar pattern when the disciples and the people witnessed one of Jesus' miracles, then they were afraid and amazed. Mark's question by the disciples, *"Teacher, do you not care that we are perishing?"* seemed out of place, because of Jesus' presence in the boat with them, unless they were concerned that he was asleep and not helping to keep the boat from sinking. Matthew (Mt 8.23-27) softened the question by saying, "Lord, save us! We are perishing!" And later Jesus' words here, *"Have you still no faith"* became, "Why are you afraid, you of little faith." As they sensed God's presence and power in Jesus, they asked, *"Who then is this, that even the wind and the sea obey him?"*

Chapter 4 Study Guide

1. Explain the parable of the sower.
2. Explain the contrasting attitudes between the parable of the sower and the parable of the lamp.

3. What are the meanings of the parables of the seed growing secretly and the mustard seed?
4. What message did Mark convey to the reader in this chapter?
5. State the purpose for Jesus calming the sea.

Chapter 5
Preaching tour, 5.1-43
The Gerasene demoniac, 5.1-20
(Mt 8.28-34; Lk 8.26-39)

Mark. They came to the other side of the sea, to the country of the Gerasenes.[a] [2] And when he had stepped out of the boat, immediately a man out of the tombs with an unclean spirit met him. [3]He lived among the tombs; and no one could restrain him any more, even with a chain; [4] for he had often been restrained with shackles and chains, but the chains he wrenched apart, and the shackles he broke in pieces; and no one had the strength to subdue him. [5]Night and day among the tombs and on the mountains he was always howling and bruising himself with stones. [6] When he saw Jesus from a distance, he ran and bowed down before him; [7] and he shouted at the top of his voice,

Demoniac. "What have you to do with me, Jesus, Son of the Most High God? I adjure you by God, do not torment me."

Mark. [8]For he had said to him,

Jesus. "Come out of the man, you unclean spirit!"

Mark. [9b] Then Jesus asked him,

Jesus. "What is your name?"

---

[a] Other ancient authorities read *Gergesenes*; others, *Gadarenes*
[b] Gk *he*

Mark. He replied,

Demoniac. "My name is Legion; for we are many."

Mark. ¹⁰ He begged him earnestly not to send them out of the country. ¹¹ Now there on the hillside a great herd of swine was feeding; ¹² and the unclean spirits[c] begged him,

Demoniac, "Send us into the swine; let us enter them."

Mark. ¹³So he gave them permission. And the unclean spirits came out and entered the swine; and the herd, numbering about two thousand, rushed down the steep bank into the sea, and were drowned in the sea.
¹⁴The swineherds ran off and told it in the city and in the country. Then people came to see what it was that had happened. ¹⁵ They came to Jesus and saw the demoniac sitting there, clothed and in his right mind, the very man who had had the legion; and they were afraid. ¹⁶Those who had seen what had happened to the demoniac and to the swine reported it. ¹⁷ Then they began to beg Jesus[d] to leave their neighborhood. ¹⁸ As he was getting into the boat, the man who had been possessed by demons begged him that he might be with him. ¹⁹ But Jesus[e] refused, and said to him,

Jesus. "Go home to your friends, and tell them how much the Lord has done for you, and what mercy he has shown you."

Mark. ²⁰And he went away and began to proclaim in the Decapolis how much Jesus had done for him; and everyone was amazed.

---

[c] Gk *they*
[d] Gk *him*
[e] Gk *he*

Jairus' daughter raised, 5.21-43
(Mt 9.18-26; 8.40-56)

Mark. [21] When Jesus had crossed again in the boat[f] to the other side, a great crowd gathered around him; and he was by the sea. [22] Then one of the leaders of the synagogue named Jairus came and, when he saw him, fell at his feet [23] and begged him repeatedly,

Jairus. "My little daughter is at the point of death. Come and lay your hands on her, so that she may be made well, and live."

Mark. [24]So he went with him.

And a large crowd followed him and pressed in on him. [25]Now there was a woman who had been suffering from hemorrhages for twelve years. [26]She had endured much under many physicians, and had spent all that she had; and she was no better, but rather grew worse. [27] She had heard about Jesus, and came up behind him in the crowd and touched his cloak, [28] for she said,

Woman. "If I but touch his clothes, I will be made well."

Mark. [29]Immediately her hemorrhage stopped; and she felt in her body that she was healed of her disease. [30] Immediately aware that power had gone forth from him, Jesus turned about in the crowd and said,

Jesus. "Who touched my clothes?"

Mark. [31]And his disciples said to him,

Disciples. You see the crowd pressing in on you; how can you say,

Jesus. 'Who touched me?'"

---

[f] Other ancient authorities lack *in the boat*

Mark. ³² He looked all around to see who had done it. ³³ But the woman, knowing what had happened to her, came in fear and trembling, fell down before him, and told him the whole truth. ³⁴ He said to her,

Jesus. "Daughter, your faith has made you well; go in peace, and be healed of your disease."

Mark. ³⁵While he was still speaking, some people came from the leader's house to say,

People from Jairus' House. "Your daughter is dead. Why trouble the teacher any further?"

Mark. ³⁶But overhearing^{gg} what they said, Jesus said to the leader of the synagogue,

Jesus. "Do not fear, only believe."

Mark. ³⁷ He allowed no one to follow him except Peter, James, and John, the brother of James. ³⁸When they came to the house of the leader of the synagogue, he saw a commotion, people weeping and wailing loudly. ³⁹When he had entered, he said to them,

Jesus. "Why do you make a commotion and weep? The child is not dead but sleeping."

Mark. ⁴⁰And they laughed at him. Then he put them all outside, and took the child's father and mother and those who were with him, and went in where the child was. ⁴¹ He took her by the hand and said to her,

Jesus. "Talitha cum,"

Mark. which means,

---

^{g} Or *ignoring*; other ancient authorities read *hearing*

Jesus. "Little girl, get up!"

Mark. [42] And immediately the girl got up and began to walk about (she was twelve years of age). At this they were overcome with amazement. [43] He strictly ordered them that no one should know this, and told them to give her something to eat.

Chapter 5 Notes
The Gerasene demoniac, 5.1-20

1: *Gadarenes* were the inhabitants of the city, or of the surrounding district, of Gadara, the capital of Perea. **2:** The man who met Jesus lived in the *tombs, and no one could restrain him any more, even with a chain* (Mt 8.28-34; Lk 8.26-39). In ancient times, mental illness was often described in terms of demon possession and the healing, by Jesus, took the form of exorcism. **3-5:** Here Jesus cured this tormented man who was so strong *that no one had the strength to subdue him.* **7:** *Do not torment me* reflected the popular belief that demons would be overthrown by God and his helpers as a prelude to the renewal of the world (Testament of Asher, 1.9; 6.2; Testament of Benjamin, 5.2; Testament of Daniel, 1.6-7; Testament of Issachar, 4.4; Testament of Judah, 13.3; 14.2; Testament of Levi, 19.1; Testament of Naphtali, 2.6; 3.1). **8-13:** Under the influence of the unclean spirit, he *and the unclean spirits begged* to enter a herd of swine. Because they could only exist in human or animal bodies, the demons' requests were granted. Mark identified the size of the heard as *numbering about two thousand* and the herd rushed *down the steep bank into the sea, and were drowned in the sea.*

14-18: The *swineherds* who lost the swine *ran off and told* what happened in the *city,* located east of the Jordan River, *and in the country,* with a predominantly non-Jewish population, who would have had no problems raising swine. When the *people came out to see Jesus,* they found the man *clothed and in his right mind.* Matthew and Mark said they begged Jesus to leave their neighborhood. Luke added that the people were seized with great fear to explain their reason for requesting Jesus to go away. **19-20:** The healed man wanted to go with Jesus, but he was told to *go home to* his *friends, and tell how much the Lord has done for* him. Mark reported that he did this *"in the Decapolis,"* a league of Hellenistic cities not mentioned in Luke. Jesus did not follow the usual command for those healed to keep the matter a secret, but to share what God had done for him.

Jairus' daughter raised, 5.21-43

21-23: Mark liked to build one story into the context of another, a practice followed by Luke in his use of Mark. Luke said Jesus got into the boat and returned, but he did not tell us where he returned. Mark identified that they crossed the Sea of Galilee again, into Jewish territory, possibility to the vicinity of Capernaum, where he met *Jairus, a leader of the synagogue.* Jairus begged *repeatedly* for Jesus to heal his daughter *who was dying.* Luke added to Mark's version and identified the girl as his *only daughter, about twelve years old.* **24-34:** On the way to Jairus' house Jesus encountered a woman who for over twelve years *had endured much under many physicians, and spent all that she had.* It was possible that Mark shared the opinion of *Mishnah Qiddushin,* 4.14, "the best among physicians is worthy of Gehenna." *She was no better, but grew worse* brought to mind the account of Tobit, "I went to physicians to be healed, but the more they treated me with ointments the more my vision was obscured" (Tobit 2.10). She *touched his cloak.* Matthew and Luke were more specific in that she touched the fringe, or sacred tassel fastened by a blue thread to each of the four corners of the outer cloak (Num 15.38-39; Duet 22.12). The cloak served as clothing during the day and as a blanket at night. The tassels were intended to remind the Israelites of their obligations to the law. The loose end of the cloak would have hung over Jesus' left shoulder, and the tassel attached to it could have been touched by anyone who *came up behind him.* **31:** Mark had the disciples answer Jesus with *"you see the crowd pressing in on you; how can you say, 'Who touched me?'"* Luke made Peter ask the question, and Jesus said, "I noticed that power had gone out from me" (Lk 8.46). **33:** The woman came forward *with fear and trembling* in part because she was in awe of Jesus and in part because of her bold action as an unclean person. She *told him the whole truth* about *what happened to her.* She was told that her *faith* had healed her and to *go in peace,* a Semitic benediction (1 Sam 1.17; 29.7).

35-38: The account of Jairus' daughter continued as *some people from the leader's house say, "Your daughter is dead"* (*see* People from Jairus' house). *A great commotion, people weeping and wailing loudly* reflected the Israelite practice that "even the poorest should hire no less than two flutes and one wailing woman" (*Mishnah Ketuboth,* 4.14; Mt 11.17; Lk 7.32). Jesus dismissed the crowd in the house and took with him *Peter, John and James,* and they entered the house with him. **39-41:** Jesus diagnosed her apparent death as a coma, and the mourners laughed. In Luke's gospel, the disciples and parents laughed. At Jesus' command, *she got up and began to walk about.* The remark *she was twelve years of age* was intended to show that the daughter was not an infant. Jesus then directed them *to give her something to eat.* **42-43:** The amazed parents were told *to tell no one what had happened.*

Chapter 5 Study Guide

1. What was the purpose of the story of the Gerasene demoniac?
2. Why send the demons into a herd of swine?
3. Explain why Jairus could believe that Jesus could heal but not raise his daughter from the dead.
4. What does, "If I but touch his clothes, I will be made well," mean to you?
5. Would it be realistic to keep quiet about Jairus' daughter being raised from the dead?

Chapter 6
Rejection at home, 6.1-6
(Mt 13.53-58; Lk 4.16-30)

Mark. [Q₁][He left that place and came to his hometown, and his disciples followed him.] ² On the sabbath he began to teach in the synagogue, and many who heard him were astounded. They said,

Synagogue members. "Where did this man get all this? What is this wisdom that has been given to him? What deeds of power are being done by his hands! ³ Is not this the carpenter, the son of Mary[a] and brother of James and Joses and Judas and Simon, and are not his sisters here with us?"

Mark. And they took offense[b] at him. ⁴ Then Jesus said to them,

Jesus. "Prophets are not without honor, except in their hometown, and among their own kin, and in their own house."

Mark. ⁵And he could do no deed of power there, except that he laid his hands on a few sick people and cured them. ⁶ And he was amazed at their unbelief.

Commissioning and instruction of the Twelve, 6.7-13
(Mt 10.1, 9-11, 14; Lk 9.1-6)

Mark. Then he went about among the villages teaching. ⁷ He called the twelve and began to send them out two by two, and gave them authority over the unclean spirits. [Q₁][⁸ He ordered them to take nothing for their journey except a staff; no bread, no bag, no money in their belts; ⁹ but to wear sandals and not to put on two tunics.] ¹⁰He said to them,

---

[a] Other ancient authorities read *son of the carpenter and of Mary*
[b] Or *stumbled*

67

Jesus. [Q₁]["Wherever you enter a house, stay there until you leave the place. ¹¹ If any place will not welcome you and they refuse to hear you, as you leave, shake off the dust that is on your feet as a testimony against them."]

Mark. [Q₁][¹² So they went out and proclaimed that all should repent. ¹³ They cast out many demons, and anointed with oil many who were sick and cured them.]

Death of John, 6.14-29
Mt 14.1-12; Lk 9.7-9)

Mark. ¹⁴ King Herod heard of it, for Jesus'ᶜ name had become known. Some wereᵈ saying,

Scoffers. "John the baptizer has been raised from the dead; and for this reason these powers are at work in him."

Mark. ¹⁵But others said,

Scoffers. "It is Elijah."

Mark. And others said,

Scoffers. "It is a prophet, like one of the prophets of old."

Mark. ¹⁶But when Herod heard of it, he said,

Herod. "John, whom I beheaded, has been raised."

Mark. ¹⁷ For Herod himself had sent men who arrested John, bound him, and put him in prison on account of Herodias, his brother

---

ᶜ Gk *his*
ᵈ Other ancient authorities read *He was*

Philip's wife, because Herod[e] had married her. [18] For John had been telling Herod,

John the Baptist. "It is not lawful for you to have your brother's wife."

Mark. [19]And Herodias had a grudge against him, and wanted to kill him. But she could not, [20]for Herod feared John, knowing that he was a righteous and holy man, and he protected him. When he heard him, he was greatly perplexed;[f] and yet he liked to listen to him. [21] But an opportunity came when Herod on his birthday gave a banquet for his courtiers and officers and for the leaders of Galilee. [22] When his daughter Herodias[g] came in and danced, she pleased Herod and his guests; and the king said to the girl,

Herod. "Ask me for whatever you wish, and I will give it.

Mark. [23]And he solemnly swore to her,

Herod. Whatever you ask me, I will give you, even half of my kingdom."

Mark. [24]She went out and said to her mother,

Salome. "What should I ask for?"

Mark. She replied,

Herodias. "The head of John the baptizer."

Mark. [25]Immediately she rushed back to the king and requested,

Salome. "I want you to give me at once the head of John the Baptist on a platter."

---

[e] Gk *he*
[f] Other ancient authorities read *he did many things*
[g] Other ancient authorities read *the daughter of Herodias herself*

Mark. [26]The king was deeply grieved; yet out of regard for his oaths and for the guests, he did not want to refuse her. [27] Immediately the king sent a soldier of the guard with orders to bring John's[h] head. He went and beheaded him in the prison, [28] brought his head on a platter, and gave it to the girl. Then the girl gave it to her mother. [29] When his disciples heard about it, they came and took his body, and laid it in a tomb.

Five thousand fed, 6.30-44
(Mt 14.13-21; Lk 9.10-17; Jn 6.1-13

Mark. [30]The apostles gathered around Jesus, and told him all that they had done and taught. [31] He said to them,

Jesus. "Come away to a deserted place all by yourselves and rest a while."

Mark. For many were coming and going, and they had no leisure even to eat. [32] And they went away in the boat to a deserted place by themselves. [33] Now many saw them going and recognized them, and they hurried there on foot from all the towns and arrived ahead of them. [34]As he went ashore, he saw a great crowd; and he had compassion for them, because they were like sheep without a shepherd; and he began to teach them many things. [35] When it grew late, his disciples came to him and said,

Disciples. "This is a deserted place, and the hour is now very late; [36] send them away so that they may go into the surrounding country and villages and buy something for themselves to eat."

Mark. [37] But he answered them,

Jesus. "You give them something to eat."

---

[h] Gk *his*

Mark. They said to him,

Disciples. "Are we to go and buy two hundred denarii[i] worth of bread, and give it to them to eat?"

Mark. [38]And he said to them,

Jesus. "How many loaves have you? Go and see."

Mark. When they had found out, they said,

Disciples. "Five, and two fish."

Mark. [39] Then he ordered them to get all the people to sit down in groups on the green grass. [40]So they sat down in groups of hundreds and of fifties. [41] Taking the five loaves and the two fish, he looked up to heaven, and blessed and broke the loaves, and gave them to his disciples to set before the people; and he divided the two fish among them all. [42] And all ate and were filled; [43] and they took up twelve baskets full of broken pieces and of the fish. [44] Those who had eaten the loaves numbered five thousand men.

Jesus walks on the water, 6.45-52
(Mt 14.22-32; Jn 6.15-21)

Mark. [45]Immediately he made his disciples get into the boat and go on ahead to the other side, to Bethsaida, while he dismissed the crowd. [46] After saying farewell to them, he went up on the mountain to pray.
    [47]When evening came, the boat was out on the sea, and he was alone on the land. [48]When he saw that they were straining at the oars against an adverse wind, he came towards them early in the morning, walking on the sea. He intended to pass them by. [49]But when they saw him walking on the sea, they thought it was a ghost and cried

---

[i] The denarius was the usual day's wage for a laborer

out; [50]for they all saw him and were terrified. But immediately he spoke to them and said,

Jesus. "Take heart, it is I; do not be afraid."

Mark. [51] Then he got into the boat with them and the wind ceased. And they were utterly astounded, [52]for they did not understand about the loaves, but their hearts were hardened.

Belief in Jesus' power to heal, 6.53-56
(Mt 14.34-36)

Mark. [53]When they had crossed over, they came to land at Gennesaret and moored the boat. [54]When they got out of the boat, people at once recognized him, [55]and rushed about that whole region and began to bring the sick on mats to wherever they heard he was. [56]And wherever he went, into villages or cities or farms, they laid the sick in the marketplaces, and begged him that they might touch even the fringe of his cloak; and all who touched it were healed.

Chapter 6 Notes
Rejection at home, 6.1-6

1-2: Jesus' visit to his *hometown* was for more than a family visit, it was to *teach* the people about the kingdom of God. The peoples' reaction was *"where did this man get all this"*, implying that he was not properly educated. Even if he had been, the message seemed different from what had been presented, because they said, *"What is this wisdom that had been given to him?"* They must have heard of some of the deeds of power performed by their childhood neighbor, even if he only preformed a limited number there (v 5). **3:** To be identified as *the son of Mary,* or of his mother, was considered an insult. Or this could be a later reaction to the doctrine of the virgin birth. The names of Jesus' four brothers are listed here, *James, Joses, Judas and Simon,* but not his sisters'. **4:** The phrase, *they took offense*

The Gospel of Mark in Dialogue

at him, should be interpreted, that they were offended by him or by what he taught them? **5:** He did *no deed of power* except for a *few* that were healed.

Commissioning and instruction of the Twelve, 6.7-13

7-13: We are not told if the Twelve were ever sent out *two by two* on more than one missionary journey, but there existed no reason to doubt they were to be an extension of Jesus' ministry. The details of the mission were vague, only that they were given *authority over the unclean spirits.* In Luke (Lk 10.17), the "seventy" reported to Jesus upon returning from their mission, "Lord, in your name even the demons submit to us!" Yet that Jesus transferred personal *power and authority* to his followers appeared to be an ecclesiastical theory. If the power was given to them, was it temporary and why were they unable to heal the epileptic child (Lk 9.37-42)? **8-9:** Mark permitted the disciples to take a *staff* and *sandals* but these were forbidden in Luke. The *bag* was used to carry extra provisions and the *two tunics* were shirts or undergarments. **10-11:** They were not to accept hospitality from more than one host in a community and not to waste any time on those *who do not welcome you.* To *shake the dust off your feet as a testimony against them* became a gesture by which a city was declared to have no part in the true Israel (cf Acts 13.51). Mark's use of these instructions might have been regarding the rejection of Jesus at his hometown or they may have reflected the attitudes of early Christians in their dealings with the Jewish.

Death of John, 6.14-29

14: *King Herod* Antipas, son of Herod the *Great* was tetrarch or prince of Galilee and Perea (Trans-Jordan). His mother was a Samaritan named Malthace, and he governed until his death in 39 CE. Herod *heard* reports about *Jesus* because his fame was growing, and he heard reports that *some thought* Jesus was *John the Baptist* raised *from the dead.* In Matthew's gospel, Herod thought Jesus was

73

John the Baptist raised *from the dead.* Although John did not perform the miracles that Jesus did, Herod, who must have believed John to be a holy person, thought that Jesus was John who *had been raised from the dead.* **15-16:** Herod divorced his first wife, the daughter of Aretas, to marry Herodias. While the law allowed the divorce it was against the law to marry *his brother's wife* while his brother was alive (Lev 18.16; 20.21). Josephus said that Herod arrested John because he was jealous of his influence over the *crowd* and *because they regarded him as Elijah* or *a prophet.* Elijah was expected to come again, by both Jews and Samaritans, before the Messianic era (Mal 4.5).

19-20: Mark stated *Herodias had a grudge against* John, *and wanted to kill him,* but Herod liked to *"listen to him."* **21:** *Birthday banquet for his courtiers, officers and leaders of Galilee* included all of the important people. **22:** It is not as clear in the NRSV, as in other Bible versions that *Herodias' daughter* was Salome (Josephus, *Jewish Antiquities,* X.Viii.5.4). **27:** According to Josephus (*The History of the Jewish War,* 7, 6, 2), John was imprisoned at Machaerus, a fortress near the Dead Sea and was beheaded there. Later Herod's army was destroyed by Aretas, and it was considered by the people just punishment for what he had done to John the Baptist. It was against Jewish law to execute a person without a trial, and execution by beheading was not permitted, but it was in accordance with Roman and Greek customs. **29:** Matthew had John's disciples telling Jesus about his death after they buried his body.

Five thousand fed, 6.30-44

30: Each of the gospel writers had their own version of this story (Mt 14.13-21; Luke 9.10-17; Jn 6.1-13). John drew upon both the feeding of the five thousand and the four thousand with the writings of Mark and Matthew. His barley loaves (Jn 6.9) reminded one of Elisha's stories (2 Kings 4.42-44), and if combined with 1 Kings (1 Kings 17.9-16) it may have provided a pattern for the gospel stories. The Jewish Talmud contained a miracle story of a similar nature. Mark reported that the *apostles gathered around Jesus* and provided him with an account of their missionary tour. **31-32:** Then Jesus took his disciples to a deserted place for a needed rest and not because of John's death. **33-34:** Many saw them and hurried to get *ahead of them. When he went ashore* and saw *the great crowd,* he was moved with compassion *because they were like sheep without a shepherd, and he began to teach them.* **35:** Since the hour for the evening meal was passed, *the disciples* wanted Jesus to dismiss the crowd in order they might *go into the surrounding country and villages and buy something for themselves to eat.* **37:** All of the synoptic writers reported Jesus' response, *"You give them something to eat"* with the disciples protesting in Mark, *"are we to go and by two hundred denarii* (a denarius was a day's wage for a laborer) *worth of bread?"* (Compare Elisha's feeding of a hundred prophets, 2 Kings 4.42-43). Luke said, "Unless we are to go and buy food for all these people." Each gospel writer reported there were *five loaves and two fish.* **39:** Mark included instructions for the *crowd to sit down* on green *grass* indicating it was spring. *Blessed and broke* suggested the prayer of praise and blessing spoken at the Last Supper and at the beginning of a Jewish meal, "Praise to you, O LORD our God, King of the Universe, you bring forth bread from the earth." **43:** *Baskets* are regarding the little food baskets that Jewish people carried so they could only eat food prepared according to the dietary laws. *Twelve* indicated that each of Twelve disciples carried one to collect the left over *broken pieces.* **45:** Matthew added "besides women and children," to convey the custom they would stand or sit separate from the men and it increased the number.

Jesus walks on the water, 6.45-52

45: *Made his disciples* may have implied that the disciples did not want to separate themselves from the excitement of the feeding of the five thousand. **46:** As was his custom, Jesus went *up the mountain to pray* (1.35; 3.13) to remain focused upon his purpose (4.1-11).

48: *Straining at the oars against an adverse wind* indicated the disciples were exhausted. *Early in the morning,* was in the Greek literally "in the fourth watch of the night" (from 3 to 6 a.m.). The Jewish people divided the night into three watches. *He intended to pass them by* seemed strange, but they saw him *walking on the sea.* **49:** In the OT, it was believed that *ghosts* or shades were lifeless creatures without any power to do good or evil. However, the popular belief in the Near East was that the shades of the dead could rise from the nether world to inflict harm upon the living, if they had been neglected by their family, or failed to receive the last rites of burial (Prov 21.16; Isa 19.3; 29.4). Matthew was the only one that told of Peter's unsuccessful attempt to walk *on the water* (Mt 14.30). Some have used this incident to explain Peter's career, pride, fall, rescue and restoration. Matthew had three miracles occurring in this account: Jesus walking on the water, as did Peter temporarily and the wind ceasing. These were not the acts of a mere human, but the Son of God (Mk 6.51-52).

Belief in Jesus' power to heal, 6.53-56

53-56: *Gennesaret* was a district on the northwestern shore of the Sea of Galilee, which was also called the Lake of Gennesaret. This fertile plain was thickly populated. *The fringe of his cloak,* or sacred tassel, was tied by a blue thread to each of the four corners of the outer cloak (Num 15.38-39; Duet 22.12), that served as clothing during the day and as a blanket at night. The tassels were intended to remind the Israelites of their obligations to the law (9.19-21). Peter's lack of faith to walk on the water was contrasted with those who were sick and believed they would be healed, if *they might touch even the fringe of his cloak.*

Chapter 6 Study Guide

1. Why did the crowd think that Jesus was John the Baptist raised from the dead?
2. Is breaking your word worse than killing someone?

3. What is your understanding of the feeding of the five thousand, plus women and children?
4. Explain the disciples' belief in ghosts but not in the ability for Jesus to walk on water.
5. Explain your understanding of the healing touch.

Chapter 7
Tradition of the elders, 7.1-23
(Mt 15.1-20)

Mark. Now when the Pharisees and some of the scribes who had come from Jerusalem gathered around him, [2] they noticed that some of his disciples were eating with defiled hands, that is, without washing them. [3] (For the Pharisees, and all the Jews, do not eat unless they thoroughly wash their hands,[a] thus observing the tradition of the elders; [4] and they do not eat anything from the market unless they wash it;[b] and there are also many other traditions that they observe, the washing of cups, pots, and bronze kettles.[c]) [5] So the Pharisees and the scribes asked him,

Pharisees and Scribes. "Why do your disciples not live[d] according to the tradition of the elders, but eat with defiled hands?"

Mark. [6]He said to them,

Jesus. "Isaiah prophesied rightly about you hypocrites, as it is written,

Lord. (I)('This people honors me with their lips, but their hearts are far from me; [7] in vain do they worship me, teaching human precepts as doctrines.' [e])

---

[a] Meaning of Gk uncertain
[b] Other ancient authorities read *and when they come from the marketplace, they do not eat unless they purify themselves*
[c] Other ancient authorities add *and beds*
[d] Gk *walk*
[e] Isa 29.13

Jesus. [8]You abandon the commandment of God and hold to human tradition."

Mark. [9]Then he said to them,

Jesus. "You have a fine way of rejecting the commandment of God in order to keep your tradition! [10]For Moses said,

LORD. (J)('Honor your father and your mother'; [f])

Jesus. and,

LORD. (J)('Whoever speaks evil of father or mother must surely die.' [g])

Jesus. [11]But you say that if anyone tells father or mother,

Pharisees and Scribes. 'Whatever support you might have had from me is Coban.'"

Mark. (that is, an offering to God[h])

Jesus. [12]"Then you no longer permit doing anything for a father or mother, [13]thus making void the word of God through your tradition that you have handed on. And you do many things like this."

Mark. [14]Then he called the crowd again and said to them,

Jesus. "Listen to me, all of you, and understand: [15]there is nothing outside a person that by going in can defile, but the things that come out are what defile."[i]

Mark. [17]When he had left the crowd and entered the house, his disciples asked him about the parable. [18]He said to them,

---

[f] Ex 20.12
[g] Ex 21.17
[h] Gk lacks *to God*
[i] Other ancient authorities add verse 16, *"Let anyone with ears to hear listen"*

Jesus. "Then do you also fail to understand? Do you not see that whatever goes into a person from outside cannot defile, [19] since it enters, not the heart but the stomach, and goes out into the sewer?"

Mark. (Thus he declared all foods clean.) [20]And he said,

Jesus. "It is what comes out of a person that defiles. [21]For it is from within, from the human heart, that evil intentions come: fornication, theft, murder, [22] adultery, avarice, wickedness, deceit, licentiousness, envy, slander, pride, folly. [23]All these evil things come from within, and they defile a person."

The Syrophoenician woman, 7.24-30
(Mt 15.21-28)

Mark. [24]From there he set out and went away to the region of Tyre.[j] He entered a house and did not want anyone to know he was there. Yet he could not escape notice, [25] but a woman whose little daughter had an unclean spirit immediately heard about him, and she came and bowed down at his feet. [26] Now the woman was a Gentile, of Syrophoenician origin. She begged him to cast the demon out of her daughter. [27]He said to her,

Jesus. "Let the children be fed first, for it is not fair to take the children's food and throw it to the dogs."

Mark. [28]But she answered him,

Woman. "Sir,[k] even the dogs under the table eat the children's crumbs."

Mark. [29]Then he said to her,

---

[j] Other ancient authorities add *and Sidon*
[k] Or *Lord*; other ancient authorities prefix *Yes*

Jesus. "For saying that, you may go—the demon has left your daughter."

Mark. [30]So she went home, found the child lying on the bed, and the demon gone.

Healings, 7.31-37
(Mt 15.29-31)

Mark. [31] Then he returned from the region of Tyre, and went by way of Sidon towards the Sea of Galilee, in the region of the Decapolis. [32]They brought to him a deaf man who had an impediment in his speech; and they begged him to lay his hand on him. [33]He took him aside in private, away from the crowd, and put his fingers into his ears, and he spat and touched his tongue. [34] Then looking up to heaven, he sighed and said to him,

Jesus. "Ephphatha,"

Mark. that is,

Jesus. "Be opened."

Mark. [35]And immediately his ears were opened, his tongue was released, and he spoke plainly. [36]Then Jesus[l] ordered them to tell no one; but the more he ordered them, the more zealously they proclaimed it. [37] They were astounded beyond measure, saying,

People. "He has done everything well; he even makes the deaf to hear and the mute to speak."

---

[l] Gk *he*

Chapter 7 Notes
Tradition of the elders, 7.1-23

At the climax of Jesus' ministry in Galilee, Mark presented a series of conflicts with the Pharisees and scribes. This followed the rejection of others, including those from his hometown, and even his disciples did not seem to understand. Three issues were presented: unwashed hands (1-8), and the Corban vow (9-13) that was directed to the Pharisees, while the last issue, ritual uncleanness (14-15, 17-23), was directed to the crowd. Matthew, writing to Jewish Christians, expanded on these conflicts and rearranged them, while Luke ignored them, maybe because the issues did not interest his Gentile readers. With a limited knowledge of Judaism, Mark felt the need to separate the teachings of Jesus from that of the oral traditions of the synagogue and the Pharisees.

1: Some *Pharisees,* with *some scribes* from *Jerusalem,* came to Galilee either to find fault with Jesus or to spread their beliefs into Galilee that was to become an important center of rabbinic Judaism in the next century. **2:** The prohibition *of eating* without *washing* the hands was a requirement for temple priests before participating in the sacrifices (Lev 22.1-16). However, it was not a general requirement before 100 CE when the practice was extended to the laity as they tried to build a fence around the Law (*Mishnah Aboth,* 1.1). The rational was "if it is good for the priests to be holy, it is appropriate for all the Holy People." **3-4:** These verses were provided to explain the issue to Gentile Christians and may have been a later addition since it was not included in all ancient manuscripts. *Tradition of the elders* was the oral law or tradition that became part of the Mishnah in about 300 BCE. The Pharisees believed the oral traditions were received by Moses on Sinai and were equal to the Torah. Since this was one of the differences between the Pharisees and the Sadducees, the statement *all of the Jews* would be inaccurate. **6:** The Pharisees were called *hypocrites,* because they pretended to follow God, but followed man (Mt 23.13, 15, 23, 25, 27, 29). **8:** Jesus' response was that they abandoned *the commandment of God* in order to *hold to human tradition,* which led to the second issue, the Coban vow.

9-13: *Coban* meant gift, that was a temple offering. Property that might be used to help a person's *father* or *mother* could be called a *Coban* that was designated for the temple and thereby released him from the obligation of caring for his parents. This vow in Jesus' time was changed by the rabbis by 100 CE where "Honor your father and your mother" (Ex 20.12) took precedence over several Jewish laws. *Gospel of the Nazaraeans,* 12, *"The Jewish Gospel has: Corban is what you should gain from us."*

14-15: In response, Jesus addressed *the crowd* expressing that it was what comes out of a person that defiled a person, not what went in. If these words of Jesus had been accepted by all the followers of Jesus, there would have been no problems later (Acts 10.1-29; Gal 3.19-29). **17-19:** The disciples did not understand and had to be instructed in private when they *entered the house* (4.10, 34; 10.10). **21-23:** This list may have been an addition to the gospel, because they are characteristic of Hellenistic rather than Jewish teachings, but they are found in Romans (Rom 1.29-31) and Galatians (Gal 5.19-23).

The Syrophoenician Woman, 7.24-30

This section of Mark's gospel was one of the most difficult to understand, as it seemed to show that Jesus was willing to extend his healing ministry to the Gentiles at *Tyre and Sidon.* This came directly after his conflict with the Pharisees, leading some to believe that it reflected the attitudes of the early church and Paul, "To the Jew first and also to the Greeks" (Rom 1.16). Matthew did not help when he inserted, "I was only sent to the lost sheep of the house of Israel" (Mt 15.24).

24: It was not the custom for a Jewish person to enter the house of a Gentile, and it seemed that Jesus *did not want anyone to know he was there.* **25:** The *woman was a Gentile of Syropheonician origin* meaning she was a Greek and probably a pagan. **27:** *The children* represented the Jewish people (cf Hos 1.10), and the *dogs,* the Gentiles. *The dogs* seemed to be rather harsh words from Jesus, but it should be understood as the common prejudices during this period, reflecting both that of the Jewish followers and Christians. Matthew seemed to believe that Jesus was only testing the woman's faith (Mt 15.24). **28:** The woman's patience and courage had to be admired as she responded, *"Even the dogs under the table eat the children's crumbs."* **29-30:** Her request was granted by Jesus and the child was healed at a distance.

Healings, 7.31-37

31-37: Jesus was moving toward the *Sea of Galilee,* but he remained in Gentile territory, when *they brought to him a deaf man* with a *speech* impediment. After just saying the word and the daughter was healed at a distance (v 30), here he took the man, removed him *from the crowd, and put his fingers into his ears, and he spat and touched his tongue.* As before, he looked up to heaven and said, "Be opened." What was noticed here was the lack of any degree of faith on the part of the deaf man, and Jesus again ordered, not only him but also those with him *to tell no one.* Maybe, Mark wanted to express, that *the more he ordered them* to tell no one, *the more zealously they proclaimed it.*

Chapter 7 Study Guide

1. What present day traditions are considered important for people of faith?
2. Why did the disciples fail to understand the conflict between Jesus and the Pharisees over the oral traditions?
3. What is your understanding of the account of the Syropheonician woman and her request to heal her daughter?
4. Explain the healing of the deaf man.
5. Why did the crowd continue to disobey Jesus and proclaim all that he had done?

Chapter 8
Four thousand fed, 8.1-10
(Mt 15.32-39)

Mark. In those days when there was again a great crowd without anything to eat, he called his disciples and said to them,

Jesus. [2]"I have compassion for the crowd, because they have been with me now for three days and have nothing to eat. [3]If I send them away hungry to their homes, they will faint on the way—and some of them have come from a great distance."

Mark. [4] His disciples replied,

Disciples. "How can one feed these people with bread here in the desert?"

Mark. [5]He asked them,

Jesus. "How many loaves do you have?"

Mark. They said,

Disciples. "Seven."

Mark. [6] Then he ordered the crowd to sit down on the ground; and he took the seven loaves, and after giving thanks he broke them and gave them to his disciples to distribute; and they distributed them to the crowd. [7] They had also a few small fish; and after blessing them, he ordered that these too should be distributed. [8] They ate and were filled; and they took up the broken pieces left over, seven baskets full. [9]Now there were about four thousand people. And he sent them away. [10]And immediately he got into the boat with his disciples and went to the district of Dalmanutha.[a]

---

[a] Other ancient authorities read *Mageda* or *Magdala*

Sayings on signs, 8.11-13
(Mt 16.1-4; 12.38-39; Lk 11.29; 11.16; 12.54-56)

Mark. [Q₂][¹¹ The Pharisees came and began to argue with him, asking him for a sign from heaven, to test him. ¹² And he sighed deeply in his spirit and said,

Jesus. "Why does this generation ask for a sign? Truly I tell you, no sign will be given to this generation."]

Mark. ¹³And he left them, and getting into the boat again, he went across to the other side.

Yeast of the Pharisees, 8.14-21
(Mt 16.5-12; Lk 12.1)

Mark. ¹⁴ Now the disciples[b] had forgotten to bring any bread; and they had only one loaf with them in the boat. ¹⁵And he cautioned them, saying,

Jesus. "Watch out—beware of the yeast of the Pharisees and the yeast of Herod."[c]

Mark. ¹⁶They said to one another,

Disciples. "It is because we have no bread."

Mark. ¹⁷And becoming aware of it, Jesus said to them,

Jesus. "Why are you talking about having no bread? Do you still not perceive or understand? Are your hearts hardened? ¹⁸ Do you have eyes, and fail to see? Do you have ears, and fail to hear? And do you not remember? ¹⁹ When I broke the five loaves for the five thousand, how many baskets full of broken pieces did you collect?"

---

[b] Gk *they*
[c] Other ancient authorities read *the Herodians*

85

Mark. They said to him,

Disciples. "Twelve."

Jesus. [20] "And the seven for the four thousand, how many baskets full of broken pieces did you collect?"

Mark. And they said to him,

Disciples. "Seven."

Mark. [21]Then he said to them,

Jesus. "Do you not yet understand?"

A blind man healed, 8.22-26
(10.46-52; Jn 9.1-7)

Mark. [22] They came to Bethsaida. Some people[d] brought a blind man to him and begged him to touch him. [23] He took the blind man by the hand and led him out of the village; and when he had put saliva on his eyes and laid his hands on him, he asked him,

Jesus. "Can you see anything?"

Mark. [24]And the man looked up and said,

Blind. "I can see people, but they look like trees, walking."

Mark. [25]Then Jesus[e] laid his hands on his eyes again; and he looked intently and his sight was restored, and he saw everything clearly. [26]Then he sent him away to his home, saying,

Jesus. "Do not even go into the village."[f]

---

[d] Gk *They*
[e] Gk *he*
[f] Other ancient authorities add *or tell anyone in the village*

Peter's confession, 8.27-38
(Mt 16.13-20; Lk 9.18-22)

Mark. [27] Jesus went on with his disciples to the villages of Caesarea Philippi; and on the way he asked his disciples,

Jesus. "Who do people say that I am?"

Mark. [28]And they answered him,

Disciples. "John the Baptist; and others, Elijah; and still others, one of the prophets."

Mark. [29]He asked them,

Jesus. "But who do you say that I am?"

Mark. Peter answered him,

Peter. "You are the Messiah."[g]

Mark. [30]And he sternly ordered them not to tell anyone about him. [31]Then he began to teach them that the Son of Man must undergo great suffering, and be rejected by the elders, the chief priests, and the scribes, and be killed, and after three days rise again. [32]He said all this quite openly. And Peter took him aside and began to rebuke him. [33]But turning and looking at his disciples, he rebuked Peter and said,

Jesus. "Get behind me, Satan! For you are setting your mind not on divine things but on human things."

---

[g] Or *the Christ*

On discipleship, 8.34-9.1
(Mt 16.24-28; Lk 9.23-27)

Mark. [34] He called the crowd with his disciples, and said to them,

Jesus. [Q$_1$]["If any want to become my followers, let them deny themselves and take up their cross and follow me. [35] For those who want to save their life will lose it, and those who lose their life for my sake, and for the sake of the gospel,[h] will save it.] [36] For what will it profit them to gain the whole world and forfeit their life? [37] Indeed, what can they give in return for their life? **[Q$_2$]**[[38] Those who are ashamed of me and of my words[i] in this adulterous and sinful generation, of them the Son of Man will also be ashamed when he comes in the glory of his Father with the holy angels."]

Chapter 8 Notes
Four thousand fed, 8.1-10

1-10: There were several common points between the feeding of the five thousand (Mt 14.13-21; Mk 6.30-44; Lk 9.10-17) and the feeding of the four thousand (Mt 15.32-39): a deserted place; little food except for a few *loaves* and *fish;* the crowd sitting down to eat; the thanks and breaking of bread; and the food left over. However, there were several differences, beginning here with Jesus *not* wanting *to send them away hungry;* the *seven baskets* full of leftovers; and *four thousand people* with Matthew adding "besides women and children." Jesus' motives in this account were clearly stated, one of sympathy, and fearing that they *might faint on the way,* if he sent them away. Jesus was moved to feed them rather than to tell the disciples to do so (Mt 14.16; Mk 6.37; Lk 9.13). **10:** *Dalmanutha* was apparently on the west side of the Sea of Galilee.

---

[h] Other ancient authorities read *lose their life for the sake of the gospel*
[i] Other ancient authorities read *and of mine*

Sayings on signs, 8.11-13

11: *A sign from heaven* was a test as it was a custom for a rabbi to be asked to provide *a sign* to prove that his teaching was true (Jn 2.18). The rabbinic commentary, *Pesikta Rabbati,* taught that when the Messiah came he would stand on the roof of the temple, and those who doubted would see a light from heaven streaming over him. *The Pharisees,* who were joined by the Sadducees in Matthew's gospel, were not concerned with the miracles he performed; they wanted *a* visible or audible *sign from heaven.* **12:** *No sign will be given to this generation* that sign would be shown to this kind of individual or group. Matthew and Luke expanded upon the reason for no sign, but Mark just indicated *he left them* meaning the Pharisees and got *into the boat again* with the disciples and crossed to the *other side.*

Yeast of the Pharisees, 8.14-21

14: While in the *boat,* it was discovered that *the disciples had forgotten to bring any bread,* and they only had *one loaf.* It provided an introduction into the disciples' lack of understanding. **15:** *The yeast of the Pharisees* was regarding their evil influence rather than their teachings. Since it was connected with *the yeast of Herod* and because Herod did not teach, Matthew changed it to "Sadducees." Yeast was a symbol of the evil impulse or wicked ways of humans. Before celebrating the seder at the Passover, all care was taken to remove all leaven bread from the house, as the power of yeast infected the new dough and spread it (Ex 12.15; 13.7). Jesus used yeast as a symbol of the kingdom of God (Mt 13.33; Lk 13.20-21) to suggest that the kingdom's influence was greater than evil. The *yeast of Herod* was not so much regarding his morality, but to his desire for glory and political privilege. **16-21:** The disciples took the reference to yeast to be because *we have no bread.* **22-23:** Jesus reminded the disciples of the feeding of the five thousand and the four thousand, and wondered why they still did *not yet understand,* even with the signs and all the teachings.

A blind man healed, 8.22-26

22: For Mark, since the disciples had not yet learned to see, or understand, about the yeast of Herod, it became necessary to perform a miracle that would open the blind man's eyes along with the disciples. **23-24:** *He led the blind man out of the village* of *Bethsaida.* This miracle was similar to 7.32 with its use of saliva and the laying on of hands. *People look like trees, walking* meant were blurred or vague. **25:** He *looked intently,* that was fixed his gaze upon something *and he saw everything clearly.* **26:** Some ancient authorities added, "or tell anyone in the village," while others read, "Go into your house and tell no one in the village," and others, "saying, 'Go into your house and if you enter the village tell no one.'"

Peter's confession, 8.27-38

27: Mark and Matthew had Jesus inquire of the disciples, *who do people say that I am,* as they were on their way to *villages of Caesarea Philippi.* The setting for Luke was after Jesus heard the report from the disciples about their missionary journey and the feeding of the five thousand with the crowd gone, this left just Jesus and his disciples. The disciples shared the same rumors told to Herod. **29:** He asked the disciples their opinion of him, *"Who do you say that I am?"* Peter, the spokesman for the disciples, identified Jesus as *"the Messiah."* Jesus accepted Peter's confession, but *he sternly ordered them not to* make it public until he reinterpreted it in terms of service, suffering and sacrifice. Matthew and Luke had "on the third day be raised" instead of Mark's *"after three days rise again."* Here Jesus became less a public figure and taught the disciples about his role as the suffering Messiah.

34-38: After his prediction of his death, resurrection, and the rebuke of Peter, Jesus taught the *disciples, and the crowd* about the cost of discipleship. His followers must *deny themselves and take up their crosses* or be willing to do away with self-concern and to be ready for self-sacrifice, even to death. **35:** To risk losing physical comfort and life, if necessary, would lead to a true life with

God. Here, *life* was not merely physical existence, but the higher or spiritual life, the real self (cf Lk 9.25; 12.15). Mark's words were for a martyr church where its members, like Jesus, must be ready to face death, if they refused to renounce Christ. Shortly after Herod the Great died, Varus crucified two thousand Jews to put down a revolt (Josephus, *Jewish Antiquities,* 17.10.10). **36:** What does it profit someone to have material success and to die without enjoying it? Compare this with the story of the rich fool (Lk 12.15-20). **37:** The apostate who renounced the faith may gain a longer physical life, and even some temporary benefits, but he would lose his life eventually and what would he say when he stood before the Son of Man?

Chapter 8 Study Guide

1. Explain the reason for the feeding of the four thousand.
2. Why is it that a physical sign must be given before some of us can believe?
3. Where was all the bread left over from the feeding of the four thousand?
4. What is meant by the yeast of the Pharisees and the yeast of Herod?
5. Why did Jesus use saliva to heal the blind man? Could this be a sign?
6. Explain why Jesus did not want the disciples to tell others that he was the Messiah.

Chapter 9

Mark. [1]And he said to them,

Jesus. "Truly I tell you, there are some standing here who will not taste death until they see that the kingdom of God has come with[a] power."

---

[a] Or *in*

The transfiguration, 9.2-8
(Mt 17.1-8; Lk 9.28-36)

Mark. ²Six days later, Jesus took with him Peter and James and John, and led them up a high mountain apart, by themselves. And he was transfigured before them, ³ and his clothes became dazzling white, such as no oneᵇ on earth could bleach them. ⁴And there appeared to them Elijah with Moses, who were talking with Jesus. ⁵Then Peter said to Jesus,

Peter. "Rabbi, it is good for us to be here; let us make three dwellings,ᶜ one for you, one for Moses, and one for Elijah."

Mark. ⁶ He did not know what to say, for they were terrified. ⁷ Then a cloud overshadowed them, and from the cloud there came a voice,

God. "This is my Son, the Beloved;ᵈ listen to him!"

Mark. ⁸Suddenly when they looked around, they saw no one with them any more, but only Jesus.

Prophecies about Elijah, 9.9-13
(Mt 17.9-13)

Mark. ⁹As they were coming down the mountain, he ordered them to tell no one about what they had seen, until after the Son of Man had risen from the dead. ¹⁰ So they kept the matter to themselves, questioning what this rising from the dead could mean. ¹¹Then they asked him,

Disciples. "Why do the scribes say that Elijah must come first?"

Mark. ¹² He said to them,

ᵇ Gk *no fuller*
ᶜ Or *tents*
ᵈ Or *my beloved Son*

Jesus. "Elijah is indeed coming first to restore all things. How then is it written about the Son of Man, that he is to go through many sufferings and be treated with contempt? ¹³ But I tell you that Elijah has come, and they did to him whatever they pleased, as it is written about him."

Epileptic child healed, 9.14-29
(Mt 17.14-21; Lk 9.37-42)

Mark. ¹⁴When they came to the disciples, they saw a great crowd around them, and some scribes arguing with them. ¹⁵ When the whole crowd saw him, they were immediately overcome with awe, and they ran forward to greet him. ¹⁶ He asked them,

Jesus. "What are you arguing about with them?"

Mark. ¹⁷Someone from the crowd answered him,

Father. "Teacher, I brought you my son; he has a spirit that makes him unable to speak; ¹⁸ and whenever it seizes him, it dashes him down; and he foams and grinds his teeth and becomes rigid; and I asked your disciples to cast it out, but they could not do so."

Mark. ¹⁹He answered them,

Jesus. "You faithless generation, how much longer must I be among you? How much longer must I put up with you? Bring him to me."

Mark. ²⁰ And they brought the boy[e] to him. When the spirit saw him, immediately it convulsed the boy,[f] and he fell on the ground and rolled about, foaming at the mouth. ²¹Jesus[g] asked the father,

Jesus. "How long has this been happening to him?"

---

[e] Gk *him*
[f] Gk *him*
[g] Gk *He*

Mark. And he said,

Father. "From childhood. [22] It has often cast him into the fire and into the water, to destroy him; but if you are able to do anything, have pity on us and help us."

Mark. [23] Jesus said to him,

Jesus. "If you are able!—All things can be done for the one who believes."

Mark. [24] Immediately the father of the boy cried out, [h]

Father. "I believe; help my unbelief!"

Mark. [25] When Jesus saw that a crowd came running together, he rebuked the unclean spirit, saying to it,

Jesus. "You spirit that keeps this boy from speaking and hearing, I command you, come out of him, and never enter him again!"

Mark. [26] After crying out and convulsing him terribly, it came out, and the boy was like a corpse, so that most of them said,

Crowd. "He is dead."

Mark. [27] But Jesus took him by the hand and lifted him up, and he was able to stand. [28] When he had entered the house, his disciples asked him privately,

Disciples. "Why could we not cast it out?"

Mark. [29] He said to them,

---

[h] Other ancient authorities add *with tears*

Jesus. "This kind can come out only through prayer."[i]

The Passion foretold again, 9.30-32
(Mt 17.22-23; Lk 9.43-45)

Mark. [30] They went on from there and passed through Galilee. He did not want anyone to know it; [31] for he was teaching his disciples, saying to them,

Jesus. "The Son of Man is to be betrayed into human hands, and they will kill him, and three days after being killed, he will rise again."

Mark. [32] But they did not understand what he was saying and were afraid to ask him.

True greatness, 9.33-37
(Mt 18.1-5; Lk 9.46-48)

Mark. [33] Then they came to Capernaum; and when he was in the house he asked them,

Jesus. "What were you arguing about on the way?"

Mark. [34] But they were silent, for on the way they had argued with one another who was the greatest. [35] He sat down, called the twelve, and said to them,

Jesus. "Whoever wants to be first must be last of all and servant of all."

Mark. [36] Then he took a little child and put it among them; and taking it in his arms, he said to them,

---

[i] Other ancient authorities add *and fasting*

Jesus. [Q₂][[37] "Whoever welcomes one such child in my name welcomes me, and whoever welcomes me welcomes not me but the one who sent me."]

The unknown exorcist, 9.38-41
(Lk 9.49-50)

Mark. [38]John said to him,

John. "Teacher, we saw someone[j] casting out demons in your name, and we tried to stop him, because he was not following us."

Mark. [39]But Jesus said,

Jesus. "Do not stop him; for no one who does a deed of power in my name will be able soon afterward to speak evil of me. **[Q₂][**[40] Whoever is not against us is for us.] [41] For truly I tell you, whoever gives you a cup of water to drink because you bear the name of Christ will by no means lose the reward.

Warnings of hell, 9.42-48
(Mt 18.6-9; 5.29-30; Lk 17.1-2)

Jesus. [Q₂][[42] "If any of you put a stumbling block before one of these little ones who believe in me,[k] it would be better for you if a great millstone were hung around your neck and you were thrown into the sea.] [43] If your hand causes you to stumble, cut it off; it is better for you to enter life maimed than to have two hands and to go to hell,[l] to the unquenchable fire.[m] [45] And if your foot causes you to stumble, cut it off; it is better for you to enter life lame than to have two feet

---

[j] Other ancient authorities add *who does not follow us*
[k] Other ancient authorities lack *in me*
[l] Gk *Gehenna*
[m] Verses 44 and 46 (which are identical with verse 48) are lacking in the best ancient authorities

and to be thrown into hell.[n][o] [47] And if your eye causes you to stumble, tear it out; it is better for you to enter the kingdom of God with one eye than to have two eyes and to be thrown into hell,[p] [48] where their worm never dies, and the fire is never quenched."

Salty disciples, 9.49-50
(Mt 5.13; Lk 14.34-35)

Jesus. [Q₁][[49] "For everyone will be salted with fire.[q] [50] Salt is good; but if salt has lost its saltiness, how can you season it?[r]] Have salt in yourselves, and be at peace with one another."

Chapter 9 Notes

1: This prediction concerning the kingdom of God was not fulfilled as expected and later Christians found it necessary to explain that it had been fulfilled at Pentecost. This issue might be addressed in a preliminary or partial kingdom on earth in contrast to the full or entire kingdom. The point was not the delay, but the necessity of being prepared for it at all times. *Taste* meant becoming personally acquainted with *death.*

The transfiguration, 9.2-8

This narrative appeared to describe a vision of Jesus in heavenly glory as the Messiah. After the resurrection, all Christians knew Jesus was the Messiah, but during Jesus' lifetime only a few of his followers were permitted a glimpse of what was to come with an event that began with prayer and grew into an intense religious

---

[n] Gk *Gehenna*
[o] Verses 44 and 46 (which are identical with verse 48) are lacking in the best ancient authorities
[p] Gk *Gehenna*
[q] Other ancient authorities either add or substitute *and every sacrifice will be salted with salt*
[r] or *how can you restore its saltiness?*

experience. **2:** Matthew and Mark placed this event *six days* after Peter's confession (Mk 16.16; Mk 8.29), while Luke placed it "about eight days after these sayings (Lk 9.20). *Peter, James, and* his brother *John* were the three who seemed to be the closest to Jesus. The *high mountain was* not identified, but it probably was Mount Hermon located near Caesarea Philippi and stood about 9,000 feet high. *Transfigured* was having a non-earthly appearance. **4:** *Moses* was the prototype (Deut 18.15) and *Elijah* the forerunner (Mal 4.5) of the Messiah and according to Deuteronomy (Deut 34.6) and 2 Kings (2 Kings 2.11), and both went directly into the heavens. *Moses,* the lawgiver, the traditional author of the first five books of the Bible, formed the basic authority in Jewish religion. **5-8:** *Three dwellings* should be translated "three tents" to maintain reference to the Feast of Booths, "On the fifteenth day of this seventh month, and lasting seven days, there shall be the festival of booths ... so that your generation may know that I made the people of Israel live in booths when I brought them out of the land of Egypt" (Lev 23.33-44). The Feast of Booths, a kind of American Thanksgiving, was one of three pilgrim festivals or holidays where Jews would make pilgrimages to the temple in Jerusalem with an offering. The booth or tent, by design was to be a temporary shelter and a reminder of the hardships endured during the years in the wilderness. The booth was a firm link between the spiritual and material world, constructed so that one might look through the roof at night and see the stars and recall one's reliance on the will of God in a hostile world. It was a joyful response to a special event, *"Lord, it is good for us to be here."* **5:** Jesus did not answer, but a *cloud,* the traditional symbol of God's presence, *overshadowed them. From the cloud came a voice* affirming Peter's thought that Jesus was the Messiah and they were to *listen to him* (3.17). **6:** It was then that the disciples *were overcome with fear.*

Prophecies about Elijah, 9.9-13

9-10: This event was kept silent by the disciples until after the resurrection because Jesus wanted to keep his messiahship a secret until his entry into Jerusalem. Matthew omitted Mark's statement, *"So they kept the matter to themselves, questioning what this rising from the dead could mean,"* to avoid showing the disciples lack of understanding about the resurrection. **10-13:** Elijah had a role in the final events at the end of history, but the scribes failed to recognize that Elijah had already come. *Elijah has already come* in the person of John the Baptist (1 Kings 19.2, 10).

Epileptic child healed, 9.14-29

14-16: The failure of the disciples to heal raised the question about the power of God granted to them when they were sent out to heal and preach (9.1-2). To be *epileptic* was attributed to the baleful influences of the moon, a demonic force (cf Ps 121.6). **17:** Jesus' response expressed a mood of weariness that was not easy to understand, and a *faithless and perverse generation* (Deut 32.5) would surely include more than the disciples. Facing his own death Jesus may have been concerned about the disciples' ability to proclaim the kingdom of God by their faith rather than by argument. Jesus rebuked the demon, healed the boy and gave him back to his father. **29:** Prayer to God was faith in God and contrasted with the argumentative attitude in v 14. The potency in faith rested with God and was not under the believer's control.

The Passion foretold again, 9.30-32

30-32: The burden of Jesus' teaching was on his coming, violent death and resurrection (8.31; 10.33-34; Lk 9.22). All three of the Synoptic Gospel writers reported that Jesus told the disciples a second time that *the Son of Man* was *to be betrayed into human hands.* Matthew had this warning while they were gathering, for the pilgrimage to Jerusalem for the Passover (Mt 17.22), while in Mark they were on their way to Jerusalem with Jesus *walking ahead of them.* Luke placed the second prediction while the crowds were amazed at all that he was doing (Lk 9.43b). Luke placed an emphasis upon these words of Jesus as he told the disciples to let these words sink into your ears "pay attention to what I am saying." Luke implied that the comment was not understood, because the Messiah's death was not a part of the disciples' Jewish faith, a spiritual truth yet to be revealed to them. Matthew said the disciples were greatly distressed, and Mark and Luke added that they *were afraid to ask him* about his death. Luke did not include in Jesus' prediction any comment about his death and resurrection.

True greatness, 9.33-37

33-37: Whenever Jesus spoke of the kingdom of God, people and the disciples thought of their role in it. Jesus reminded the disciples they should think of and seeking opportunities for service to God's little ones. This would change their disposition and habits to become like children, turn away from self-chosen goals, and relate oneself to God as to a father. The pagan world did not place the same value upon children as Jesus. Jesus stressed that children were objects of God's love and it was communicated to the early church (10.40-42; 25.31-46). Childlike relationships to a parent, not childish behaviors, were in view (Mk 10.15; Lk 18.17; 1 Pet 2.2). *In my name* meant "at my command" or "for my sake."

The unknown exorcist, 9.38-41

38-41: Compare the account of Eldad and Medad (Num 11.26-29) where Moses rebuked Joshua for the same jealous attitude. *Oxyrhynchus Papyrus,* 1224, fol. 2 recto, col. 1, "For the one who is not against you is for you. The one who today is far away will tomorrow be near you."

Warnings of hell, 9.42-48

42: *Little ones,* for Luke may have meant the disciples or a special group among them, Matthew and Mark added, *"who believe in me."*

A great millstone was a heavy stone that could only be turned by using an animal, and if *hung around your neck,* you would surely drown when thrown into *the sea.* **43-47:** Occasions for stumbling were bound to occur, but for those who wanted to cause others to stumble, it would be better for them to be born *maimed.* These verses were used in a figurative manner meaning that whenever temptations to control or abuse someone arose, they were to have been discarded properly and decisively (Mk 9.43-48; Mt 5.29-30), nor should they be taken to support a restriction on social relationships because of a fear to be involved with evil. Jesus had contact with sinners and for him the protection from evil rested in a commitment to God's will and a deep concern for the welfare of others. **48:** *The fire is never quenched* was a reference to the Greek: "Gehenna of fire" (Isa 66.24).

Salty disciples, 9.49-50

49-50: *Salt* was important for food preservation and taste, and as a necessity it was heavily taxed in ancient times and was frequently sold in an altered form that had decreased value. When it lost it effectiveness, it became useless. **50b:** Perhaps the meaning was, "Maintain peacefully your own distinct character and service."

Chapter 9 Study Guide

1. What is the significance of the transfiguration event?
2. Why did Peter want to make three dwellings (booths)?
3. If the end of time is so near, is it not too late for Elijah's preparatory ministry?
4. Explain the disciple's inability to heal the epileptic boy.
5. Why did Jesus feel the need to tell the disciples a second time about his death and resurrection?
6. What does the statement about salty disciples mean to you?

Chapter 10
From Galilee to Jerusalem, 10.1-52
(Mt 19.1-20.34; Lk 18.15-19.27)
On marriage and divorce, 10.1-12
(Mt 19.1-12)

Mark. He left that place and went to the region of Judea and[a] beyond the Jordan. And crowds again gathered around him; and, as was his custom, he again taught them.
[2] Some Pharisees came, and to test him they asked,

Pharisees. "Is it lawful for a man to divorce his wife?"

Mark. [3]He answered them,

Jesus. "What did Moses command you?"

Mark. [4]They said,

Pharisees. "Moses allowed a man to write a certificate of dismissal and to divorce her."

Mark. [5]But Jesus said to them,

Jesus. "Because of your hardness of heart he wrote this commandment for you. [6] But from the beginning of creation,

God. (P)('God made them male and female.' [7]'For this reason a man shall leave his father and mother and be joined to his wife,[b] [8] and the two shall become one flesh.' [c])

Jesus. So they are no longer two, but one flesh. [9]Therefore what God has joined together, let no one separate."

---

[a] Other ancient authorities lack *and*
[b] Other ancient authorities lack *and be joined to his wife*
[c] Gen 1.27

Mark. [10]Then in the house the disciples asked him again about this matter. [11] He said to them,

Jesus. [Q$_3$]["Whoever divorces his wife and marries another commits adultery against her; [12] and if she divorces her husband and marries another, she commits adultery."]

Blessing the children, 10.13-16
(Mt 19.13-15; Lk 18.15-17)

Mark. [13] People were bringing little children to him in order that he might touch them; and the disciples spoke sternly to them. [14]But when Jesus saw this, he was indignant and said to them,

Jesus. "Let the little children come to me; do not stop them; for it is to such as these that the kingdom of God belongs. [15]Truly I tell you, whoever does not receive the kingdom of God as a little child will never enter it."

Mark. [16]And he took them up in his arms, laid his hands on them, and blessed them.

The rich man, 10.17-31
(Mt 19.16-30; Lk 18.18-30)

Mark. [17]As he was setting out on a journey, a man ran up and knelt before him, and asked him,

Rich man. "Good Teacher, what must I do to inherit eternal life?"

Mark. [18]Jesus said to him,

Jesus. "Why do you call me good? No one is good but God alone. [19] You know the commandments:

LORD. (J)('You shall not murder; You shall not commit adultery; You shall not steal; You shall not bear false witness; You shall not defraud; Honor your father and mother.'" [d])

Mark. He said to him,

Rich man. [20] "Teacher, I have kept all these since my youth."

Mark. [21]Jesus, looking at him, loved him and said,

Jesus. [Q₁]["You lack one thing; go, sell what you own, and give the money[e] to the poor, and you will have treasure in heaven; then come, follow me."]

Mark. [22]When he heard this, he was shocked and went away grieving, for he had many possessions.
[23]Then Jesus looked around and said to his disciples,

Jesus. "How hard it will be for those who have wealth to enter the kingdom of God!"

Mark. [24]And the disciples were perplexed at these words. But Jesus said to them again,

Jesus. "Children, how hard it is[f] to enter the kingdom of God! [25] It is easier for a camel to go through the eye of a needle than for someone who is rich to enter the kingdom of God."

Mark. [26]They were greatly astounded and said to one another,[g]

Disciples. "Then who can be saved?"

---

[d] Ex 20.10-16
[e] Gk lacks *the money*
[e] Other ancient authorities add *for those who trust in riches*
[f] Other ancient authorities read *to him*
[g] Or *gospel*

Mark. ²⁷Jesus looked at them and said,

Jesus. "For mortals it is impossible, but not for God; for God all things are possible."

Mark. ²⁸Peter began to say to him,

Peter. "Look, we have left everything and followed you."

Mark. ²⁹Jesus said,

Jesus. "Truly I tell you, [Q₁][there is no one who has left house or brothers or sisters or mother or father or children or fields, for my sake and for the sake of the good news,ᵍ] ³⁰ who will not receive a hundredfold now in this age—houses, brothers and sisters, mothers and children, and fields, with persecutions—and in the age to come eternal life. [Q₁][³¹ But many who are first will be last, and the last will be first."]

The Passion foretold a third time, 10.32-34
(Mt 20.17-19; Lk 18.31-34)

Mark. ³²They were on the road, going up to Jerusalem, and Jesus was walking ahead of them; they were amazed, and those who followed were afraid. He took the twelve aside again and began to tell them what was to happen to him, ³³ saying,

Jesus. "See, we are going up to Jerusalem, and the Son of Man will be handed over to the chief priests and the scribes, and they will condemn him to death; then they will hand him over to the Gentiles; ³⁴ they will mock him, and spit upon him, and flog him, and kill him; and after three days he will rise again."

James and John seek honor, 10.35-45
(Mt 20.20-28; Lk 22.24-27)

Mark. [35] James and John, the sons of Zebedee, came forward to him and said to him,

James and John. "Teacher, we want you to do for us whatever we ask of you."

Mark. [36] And he said to them,

Jesus. "What is it you want me to do for you?"

Mark. [37] And they said to him,

James and John. "Grant us to sit, one at your right hand and one at your left, in your glory."

Mark. [38] But Jesus said to them,

Jesus. "You do not know what you are asking. Are you able to drink the cup that I drink, or be baptized with the baptism that I am baptized with?"

Mark. [39] They replied,

James and John. "We are able."

Mark. Then Jesus said to them,

Jesus. "The cup that I drink you will drink; and with the baptism with which I am baptized, you will be baptized; [40] but to sit at my right hand or at my left is not mine to grant, but it is for those for whom it has been prepared."

Mark. [41]When the ten heard this, they began to be angry with James and John. [42]So Jesus called them and said to them,

Jesus. "You know that among the Gentiles those whom they recognize as their rulers lord it over them, and their great ones are tyrants over them. [43] But it is not so among you; but whoever wishes to become great among you must be your servant, [44] and whoever wishes to be first among you must be slave of all. [45] For the Son of Man came not to be served but to serve, and to give his life a ransom for many."

Blind Bartimaeus, 10.46-52
(Mt 20.29-34; Lk 18.35-43)

Mark. [46]They came to Jericho. As he and his disciples and a large crowd were leaving Jericho, Bartimaeus son of Timaeus, a blind beggar, was sitting by the roadside. [47] When he heard that it was Jesus of Nazareth, he began to shout out and say,

Bartimaeus. "Jesus, Son of David, have mercy on me!"

Mark. [48] Many sternly ordered him to be quiet, but he cried out even more loudly,

Bartimaeus. "Son of David, have mercy on me!"

Mark. [49]Jesus stood still and said,

Jesus. "Call him here."

Mark. And they called the blind man, saying to him,

Disciples. "Take heart; get up, he is calling you."

Mark. [50]So throwing off his cloak, he sprang up and came to Jesus. [51] Then Jesus said to him,

Jesus. "What do you want me to do for you?"

Mark. The blind man said to him,

Bartimaeus. "My teacher,[h] let me see again."

Mark. [52]Jesus said to him,

Jesus. "Go; your faith has made you well."

Mark. Immediately he regained his sight and followed him on the way.

Chapter 10 Notes
From Galilee to Jerusalem, 10.1-52
On marriage and divorce, 10.1-12

1: *Beyond the Jordan* meant in Perea. (Lk 9.51; Jn 10.40; 11.7). Mark's, *He again taught them* was presented by Matthew as "and he cured them there" (Mt 19.2).
2: The question about divorce seemed to be presented from the Christian, rather than the Jewish viewpoint, since divorce had always been possible in Judaism. What was debated among the Pharisees was not if a man could divorce his wife, but for what cause? The school of Shammai permitted divorce only if the wife was guilty of unchastity or gross immodesty, while the school of Hillel permitted a man to divorce his wife even if she only spoiled his food. A Jewish marriage was not a contract between equals, because a woman did not marry, she was "given in marriage." **3-4:** *What did Moses command you* (Deut 24.1-4)? *Allowed a man to write a certificate of dismissal* and this was considered by the Jewish people a step forward as it allowed a woman, who as a divorcee and without protection, with a certificate to seek the protection of another man and not be accused of adultery. This certificate, referred to in the Torah as a "get," must

---

[h] Aramaic *Rabbouni*

be written on durable material with ink that would not fade and had to be placed in the wife's hand by the husband. Once it was delivered to the wife, it could not be retracted. Without a certificate, a woman could not remarry, and many Jewish men before going to war would give their wives a provisional certificate, but if the husband died without granting the certificate, the widow could not remarry (Mt 5.31-32). The divorced wife could not marry for ninety days, as a way of leaving no question in paternity cases. A wife could take her husband to court that might compel him to grant a divorce, if he had some "loathsome" disease, if he refused to support her, or to have sex with her, or where the court had ordered him to stop beating her. **5:** Jesus proclaimed that the Law was shaped to the character of those for whom it was written. *This commandment* was written *for you* because of your dull minds, uncivilized emotions, and *your hardness of heart.* **6:** Jesus pointed out that divorce was contrary to divine intention in marriage in that the *two shall become one flesh* (Gen 1.27; 2.24; 5.2). Jesus protested against the cruelty of men in divorcing their wives (Mal 2.13-16), and leaving the woman without any protection and with no choice but to be remarried.

10-11: The private discussion between Jesus and the disciples introduced some new material from Q_3 that presented the man as the active part in the divorce, *whoever divorces his wife.* **12:** Both Matthew (Mt 5.32) and Luke (Lk 16.18) omit v 12 and there was little doubt that Roman law influenced this rule, but it did not apply in Palestine, where women could not sue for divorce.

Blessing the children, 10.13-16

13-16: Placing a value on family life, Jewish parents would bring their children to have the rabbis bless them that included laying his hands on them and praying. The disciples *spoke sternly* to the parents and others, wanting to protect Jesus from what they considered trivial matters, as the *people* often made it difficult for him to function or even move. Both Matthew and Luke omit Mark's comment that Jesus *was indignant,* as well as that he embraced the children as he blessed them. *For it is to such as these that the kingdom of God belongs* meaning those who depend in trustful simplicity share in God's kingdom.

The rich man, 10.17-31

17: The ruler is usually called "the rich young ruler" resulting from the combined information from the Synoptics. Mark called him a *rich man,* and Matthew called him a young man, while Luke identified him as a ruler, a member of the governing body of a synagogue. *Gospel of the Nazaraeans,* (in Origen, *Commentary on Matthew* 15.14 in the Latin version), "The second of the rich people said to Jesus, 'Teacher, what good things can I do and live?' Jesus answered, 'Fulfill the law and the prophets.' The person answered, 'I have.' Jesus said, 'Go, sell all that you have and distribute to the poor; and come, follow me.' But the rich man began to scratch his head, for it did not please him. And the Lord said to him, 'How can you say, I have fulfilled the law and the prophets, when it is written in the law; You shall love your neighbor as yourself; and look, many of your neighbors, children of Abraham and Sarah, are covered with filth, dying of hunger, and your house is full of good things, none of which is given to them? And Jesus turned and said to Simon, the disciple, who was sitting nearby, 'Simon, son of Jonah, it is easier for a camel to go through the eye of a needle than for a rich person to enter the kingdom of heaven.'" *Gospel of the Naassenes,* (in Hippolytus, *Refutation of All Heresies,* v.7.26) read, "why do you call me good? One there is who is good – my Father who is in heaven – who makes his sun to rise on the just and on the unjust, and sends rain on the pure and on sinners" (cf 5.45). Jesus replied that the good way of life was obedience to God's will (15.2-3, 6). The Greek tense of the phrase keep the commandments implied not a single action but a continued process. *Eternal life* was to share in the life to come, the kingdom of God. The commandments in Matthew (Mt 19.18-19) were taken from Mark (Mk 10.19; Ex 20.10-16) and Jesus added, "You shall love your neighbor as yourself" (Deut 5.16-20; Rom 13.9; Jas 2.11). **18:** Mark and Luke mirrored Jesus' response regarding "good" by saying, *no one is good but God alone,* while Matthew seemed to put a different spin upon the question (Mt 19.17a), by saying "Why do you ask me about what is good (Lev 19.18; Mt 22.39; Rom 13.8; Jas 2.8-9). *"I have kept all these"* represented an honest claim. Rabbinical teachers believed that it was possible for men to fulfill their obligations to the whole law (Mt 19.20; Mk 10.20; Lk 18.21). Jesus consistently turned people's attention away from concern over their own religious standing, as he called them to involve themselves in the basic, vital interests of others. Neither wealth, poverty nor formal piety were so important as sharing in the working out of God's life-giving design for all people (Mt 5.23-24, 43-48; 6.33).

While it was difficult, many rich men became disciples such as Matthew (Mt 9.9), Joseph of Arimathea (Mt 27.57), and Zacchaeus (Lk 19.9), but this rich man, one that Mark said whom Jesus *loved* (Mk 10.21), found that discipleship would cost him too much. Luke (Lk 18.23-24) had Jesus address the rich man, while both Matthew and Mark had Jesus make the comment to the disciples.

25: The *camel* was the largest beast of burden known in Palestine. The *needle's eye* was the name of a small gate in the wall that surrounded Jerusalem, and it should not be explained away by the Greek use of the *eye of a needle* on a "rope" or "cable." **26-27:** Each of the Synoptic Gospel writers grouped together some difficult teachings presented by Jesus (Mt 19.1-25; Mk 10.1-25; Lk 18.1-25), and then for Matthew and Mark the *disciples,* while for Luke it was the crowd, who all responded with the question, *"Who then can be saved?"* It brought into focus the sharp difference between the teachings of Jesus and those of the rabbinical teachers who believed that it was possible for men to fulfill their obligations to the whole law. Jesus said, *"for mortals it is impossible"* (Mt19.26; Mk 10.27; Lk 18.27). What was impossible for man, *but for God all things are possible* (Gen 18.14; Jer 32.17).

28-31: *Peter,* the spokesman for the disciples, missed what Paul later understood, that "no human being will be justified in his sight" by deeds as prescribed by the law, for through the law come the knowledge of sin (Rom 3.20). *We have left everything* meaning the disciples were not like the rich man. *The renewal of all things* referred to the consummation of God's purpose (cf Rom 8.18-25). *Jesus* assured the disciples they would receive more in this age and in the life to come. So much for serving God without any reward, unless this was used to assure the early church that God noticed their sacrifices (Mt 20.16; 19.29-30; Mk 10.31; Lk 13.30).

The Passion foretold a third time, 10.32-34

32-34: The passion foretold a third time indicated that Jesus was now on the way to Jerusalem for the final time (cf 16.21; 17.22). Matthew and Mark reported that *the Son of Man will be handed over to the chief priest and scribes* before being handed *over to the Gentiles.* Luke just had the Son of Man being handed directly over to the Gentiles. All three Synoptic Gospel writers implied that Jesus tried to explain the passion to the disciples, but Luke clarified that "they understood nothing about these things" (Lk 18.34), and that their failure to understand was in accordance with God's purpose.

James and John seek honor, 10.35-45

35: While in Mark, James and John made the request for seats of honor, Matthew had their *mother*, Salome, make the request (*see* 27.56 and Mk 15.40-41). **22:** *Cup* was a frequent OT metaphor used to describe suffering by the hand of God (Isa 51.17). *Gospel of the Naassenes,* (in Hippolutus, *Refutation of All Heresies,* V.8.11), "But" Jesus says, "even if you drink the cup which I drink, you will not be able to enter where I go." James was the first of the Twelve to suffer martyrdom under Herod Agrippa in 44 CE (Acts 12.2) while John was believed to have died in old age at Ephesus. Jesus declared that the *Father* would assign the chief places according to the divine plan.

41: *They were angry with the brothers* meaning the ten who were afraid of losing something themselves. It also indicated that James and John either were a part of, or knew about their mother's request. **42:** *Gentiles those whom they recognize as their rulers* were probably in reference to the Romans. Greatness to the rulers meant power to dominate and dictate to others. Greatness to Jesus appeared in the ability to serve and help others (Mk 9.35). **45:** *To give his life a ransom for many* was an introduction of a new idea but did not indicate that a ransom was paid to someone, God or the devil (26.39; 1 Tim 2.5-6; Jn 13.15-16; Titus 2.14; 1 Peter 1.18). The thought seemed to be based on Isaiah (Isa 53.12) as the Suffering Servant. *Many* did not limit the number but that the benefit would be widely effective.

Blind Bartimaeus, 10.46-52

46-52: *Jericho,* a village in Judea near an important ford over the Jordan River, was used by travelers when they went from Galilee to Jerusalem by way of Perea to avoid contact with the Samaritans. Matthew reworked Mark's account of the healing of Bartimaeus where the emphasis was upon the man's persistence and where Jesus proclaimed, "Go, your faith has made you well" (v 52). Matthew omitted these details and had Jesus touch the eyes of the two blind men, with no mention of faith. **47:** The messianic title, *Son of David* was used by all three Synoptic gospel writers and it was a dangerous thing politically to have Jesus identified as King of the Jews, the Messiah. Jesus did not respond to the cries *"Son of David"*, but to *"Have mercy"* (Mk 10.48; Lk 18.39). Mark and Luke both used this title and assumed in their writings that Jesus' true nature was now in the open and the reader was prepared for the triumphal entry into Jerusalem. **48:** The blind man (*see* Blind) was told to be quiet *but shouted even more loudly.* **51:** Jesus asked, *"What do you want me to do for you?"* The response was *"Let me see again."* Matthew conveyed that Jesus was moved with compassion, so he touched the eyes of the two blind men, they regained their sight, and they followed him as disciples. In Mark, the blind man received his sight *and followed him on the way.*

Chapter 10 Study Guide

1. What is your reaction to the discourse on marriage and divorce?
2. What role did children play in Jesus' ministry?
3. Why did the rich man find it difficult to become a disciple of Jesus?
4. What is your response to the question of the disciple or the crowd, "then who can be saved?"
5. Why were the other ten disciples angry with James and John?

Chapter 11
The last week, 11.1-15.47
(Mt 21.1-27.66; Lk 19.28-23.56)
Palm Sunday, 11.1-11
(Mt 21.1-9; Lk 19.28-38)

Mark. When they were approaching Jerusalem, at Bethphage and Bethany, near the Mount of Olives, he sent two of his disciples [2] and said to them,

Jesus. "Go into the village ahead of you, and immediately as you enter it, you will find tied there a colt that has never been ridden; untie it and bring it. [3] If anyone says to you,

Bystanders. 'Why are you doing this?'

Jesus. just say this,

Disciples. 'The Lord needs it and will send it back here immediately.'"

Mark. [4] They went away and found a colt tied near a door, outside in the street. As they were untying it, [5] some of the bystanders said to them,

114

Bystanders. "What are you doing, untying the colt?"

Mark. ⁶They told them what Jesus had said; and they allowed them to take it. ⁷Then they brought the colt to Jesus and threw their cloaks on it; and he sat on it. ⁸Many people spread their cloaks on the road, and others spread leafy branches that they had cut in the fields. ⁹Then those who went ahead and those who followed were shouting,

Crowd. "Hosanna! [Q₃][Blessed is the one who comes in the name of the Lord!] ¹⁰Blessed is the coming kingdom of our ancestor David! Hosanna in the highest heaven!"

Mark. ¹¹Then he entered Jerusalem and went into the temple; and when he had looked around at everything, as it was already late, he went out to Bethany with the twelve.

Fig tree cursed, 11.12-14
(Mt 21.18-19; Lk 13.6-9)

Mark. ¹²On the following day, when they came from Bethany, he was hungry. ¹³Seeing in the distance a fig tree in leaf, he went to see whether perhaps he would find anything on it. When he came to it, he found nothing but leaves, for it was not the season for figs. ¹⁴He said to it,

Jesus. "May no one ever eat fruit from you again."

Mark. And his disciples heard it.

Cleansing the temple, 11.15-19
(Mt 21.12-13; Lk 19.45-48; Jn 2.13-17)

Mark. ¹⁵Then they came to Jerusalem. And he entered the temple and began to drive out those who were selling and those who were buying in the temple, and he overturned the tables of the money changers and the seats of those who sold doves; [16] and he would not allow anyone to carry anything through the temple. [17] He was teaching and saying,

Jesus. "Is it not written,

LORD. (T-I)('My house shall be called a house of prayer for all the nations'? [a]) **(B)**(But you have made it a den of robbers." [b])

Mark. [18] And when the chief priests and the scribes heard it, they kept looking for a way to kill him; for they were afraid of him, because the whole crowd was spellbound by his teaching. [19] And when evening came, Jesus and his disciples[c] went out of the city.

The meaning of the withered fig tree, 11.20-25
(Mt 21.18-22)

Mark. [20] In the morning as they passed by, they saw the fig tree withered away to its roots. [21] Then Peter remembered and said to him,

Peter. "Rabbi, look! The fig tree that you cursed has withered."

Mark. [22] Jesus answered them,

Jesus. [Q₂] ["Have[d] faith in God. [23] Truly I tell you, if you say to this mountain,

Disciples. 'Be taken up and thrown into the sea,'

Jesus. and if you do not doubt in your heart, but believe that what you say will come to pass, it will be done for you.] [24] So I tell you, whatever you ask for in prayer, believe that you have received[e] it, and it will be yours.

---

[a] alsa 56.7
[b] Jer 7.11
[c] Gk *they*: other ancient authorities read *he*
[d] Other ancient authorities read *"If you have*
[e] Other ancient authorities read *are receiving*

²⁵ "Whenever you stand praying, forgive, if you have anything against anyone; so that your Father in heaven may also forgive you your trespasses."ᶠ

On Jesus' authority, 11.27-33
(Mt 21.23-27; Lk 20.1-8; Jn 2.18-22)

Mark. ²⁷Again they came to Jerusalem. As he was walking in the temple, the chief priests, the scribes, and the elders came to him ²⁸ and said,

Chief priests, Scribes and Elders. "By what authority are you doing these things? Who gave you this authority to do them?"

Mark. ²⁹Jesus said to them,

Jesus. "I will ask you one question; answer me, and I will tell you by what authority I do these things. ³⁰ Did the baptism of John come from heaven, or was it of human origin? Answer me."

Mark. ³¹They argued with one another,

Chief priests, Scribes and Elders. "If we say, 'From heaven,' he will say, 'Why then did you not believe him?'

Another Argument. ³² But shall we say, 'Of human origin'?"

Mark. —they were afraid of the crowd, for all regarded John as truly a prophet. ³³So they answered Jesus,

Chief priests, Scribes and Elders. "We do not know."

Mark. And Jesus said to them,

ᶠ Other ancient authorities add verse 26, *"But if you do not forgive, neither will your Father in heaven forgive your trespasses."*

Jesus. "Neither will I tell you by what authority I am doing these things."

Chapter 11 Notes
The last week, 11.1-15.47

The next few chapters of Mark are devoted to Jesus' ministry, arrest, trial, death, burial and resurrection. Church tradition held that all of these events took place within a single week, just a few days before the Passover Festival. The Synoptic Gospels (Matthew, Mark and Luke) presented the idea that this was Jesus' first visit to Jerusalem during his ministry, yet it seemed that he had friends in the city (Mt 21.2-3; Mk 11.2-3; Lk 19.30-31), and he seemed to be known by Simon the Leper (Mt 26.6; Mk 14.3). The statement about Jerusalem by Jesus could be interpreted that Jesus had made other visits to the Holy City (Mt 23.37-39; Lk 13.34-45). John the Evangelist, in his gospel, had Jesus make several trips to Jerusalem with his disciples, most of them for festivals.

The length of stay in Jerusalem presented other issues. The triumphal entry was conventionally placed on Palm Sunday with Jesus spending the previous sabbath just east of Jericho. This would have had him arrive in Jerusalem on Sunday evening. This agreed with Mark where he went to the temple, but *"it was already late"* so *"he went out to Bethany with the twelve"* (Mk 11.11). This made the cursing of the fig tree and the cleansing of the temple take place on Monday (11.12-19). The story of the disciples calling attention to the withered fig tree then took place on Tuesday with nothing said about the end of the day (Mk 11.20-26). One may assume that the "again they came to Jerusalem" (Mk 11.27) happened on Wednesday, along with the preparation for the Passover seder or searching for the leaven, with the seder or the Last Supper being held on Thursday evening.

Then there was the cursing of the fig tree because of its lack of fruit, "When it was not the season." In Jerusalem, figs usually did not ripen until summer time and the fig trees would continue to bear fruit for ten months. Therefore, figs would be available during the fall Tabernacle Festival, but not during the spring Passover Festival. Using cut branches or foliage from trees and shouts of "Hosanna" and "Blessed is the one who comes in the name of the Lord" suggested the temple ritual during the Tabernacle Festival rather than the Passover Festival. Therefore, it could be suggested that the Triumphal Entry was part of the Tabernacle Festival while at least the seder service was part of the Passover service. Therefore, Jesus and the disciples were in Jerusalem for an extended period, or upon several occasions, when Jesus aroused the anger of the religious establishment.

At the beginning of the Christian era, a majority of the Jewish people believed in the coming of a mighty warrior-Messiah of David's line. The Qumran Community looked forward to the time when such a Messiah would lead them in the great final battle between "the sons of darkness" and the "sons of light." The Zealots were also ready at any moment to flock to the Messiah's standard and to fight by his side with naked sword. When the Messiah would come, the people would "Rejoice greatly, O daughter of Zion! Shout aloud, O daughter of Jerusalem! Lo, your king comes to you; triumphant and victorious is he, humble and riding on a donkey, on a colt, the foal of a donkey" (Zech 9.9).

Each year Jewish males from all around would make pilgrimages to Jerusalem to celebrate three major festivals; the Passover, Weeks and Booths. During these three festivals, Messianic expectations would run high among the people. Jesus was a popular figure and no stranger to many of these visitors, including the leaders of Jerusalem. When he entered the city on a donkey, the Messianic expectations took on an air of excitement.

Palm Sunday, 11.1-11

1: Jesus, while putting an emphasis on humility, offered himself as the Messiah. Like a parable, his action had to be understood and accepted (Jn 6.14; 7.40; Acts 3.22; Mk 6.15; Lk 13.33). Jesus, his disciples, and the crowd (Mt 20.29) traveled up the steep road from Jericho to *Jerusalem. Bethphage* was not mentioned before in the gospels, but it was near Bethany, less than two miles southeast of Jerusalem. **2:** Matthew had Jesus tell the *two disciples* to bring both the donkey and a colt tied with her while Mark and Luke only mentioned a *colt.* **3:** *And will send it back here immediately* suggested the owner was a secret disciple of Jesus. **8:** Mark had those who were shouting as *"many people"* and Matthew expanded the group to a very large crowd that treated Jesus as a kingly leader that was coming to take his throne. Luke identified the group as a "multitude of the disciples" meaning more than the Twelve. *Cloaks* and *cut branches* were tokens of honor (2 Kings 9.13). **9-10:** *Hosanna* originally was a Hebrew invocation addressed to God, meaning, "Save now" and was later used as a cry of joyous acclamation. *Blessed is the one who comes in the name of the Lord* (Ps 118.26; *see* LORD) was used as a greeting to pilgrims approaching the temple. *Hosanna in the highest heaven* meant either "raise the cry of hosanna to the heavens" or "God in heaven save." Jesus did not encourage the use of *Son of David* and asked his disciples to refrain from calling him the Messiah as it encouraged ideas of a political and military deliverer.

Fig tree cursed, 11.12-14

12-13: Mark reported, *"It was not the season for figs",* then why would Jesus curse the fig tree, as it seemed against his nature? Some hold that the leaves showed the possibility of green fruit and in disappointment, Jesus cursed the tree. But what should be done with the leaves of the fig tree normally appearing after the fruit? It was probable that the early church used this parable to condemn Israel for failing to produce the fruits of faith and obedience.

Cleansing the temple, 11.15-19

According to Mark, the cleansing of the temple did not take place until the next day, "as it was already late" (Mk 11.11). **15:** The animals for sale were acceptable for sacrifice; the moneychangers converted Gentile coins into Jewish money that could properly be presented in the temple (Ex 30.13; Lev 1.14). *Entered the temple,* or more specifically the large outer court called the Court of the Gentiles, the only place Gentiles were permitted. Matthew and Luke compressed Mark's account of cleaning the temple by omitting *a house of prayer for all nations.* Jesus protested the commercialization even in this one area where Gentiles could enter. Only in John's gospel were we told that Jesus made a whip of cords and used strong violence to achieve his end (Jn 2.13-17). In their desire to make a profit, the sellers reduced the *house of prayer* into *a den of robbers.*

The meaning of the withered fig tree, 11.20-25

23: Jesus emphasized not power in faith but the power in God, his illustration being figurative. Faith would command but only according to God's will (Mt 4.3-4; Mk 14.35-36). **24:** What God willed became possible both to himself and to the person who shared his will.

On Jesus' authority, 11.27-33

The Sanhedrin heard of Jesus' activities in Galilee and they were watching him with suspicion. As long as he remained in the northern providence he was under the rule of Herod Antipas, and they were restricted from taking any direct action against him. However, when he entered Judea he came under their authority, and as someone who might cause a political uprising or ignite the messianic hopes, he became a matter of their concern.

27: So, they sent a delegation of *chief priests, scribes and elders* to trap Jesus into admitting something that they could use against him before the Roman procurator. Mark had this incident happening the day after the cleansing of the temple, an act challenged by the Sanhedrin. Matthew and Luke have Jesus teaching the people in the temple, telling the good news, as the basis for the challenge of his *authority,* since he had not been trained and ordained as a rabbi. The issue was they wanted to obtain from Jesus a messianic claim. **29:** Jesus wanted to establish there was a connection between his ministry and that of John's and that his authority came *from heaven.* Their refusal to answer his question freed Jesus from having to reply to their challenges. **32:** While Mark and Matthew make their hesitation to answer because *"we are afraid of the crowd,"* Luke made the consequences more violent, "all the people will stone us."

Chapter 11 Study Guide

1. Explain some of the Messianic expectations present at the triumphal entry.
2. Why was the fig tree cursed?
3. Explain why Mark included a house of prayer "for all nations".
4. Why did the Chief Priests, Elders and Scribes question Jesus' authority?
5. Explain why the issue of John the Baptist was so difficult for the religious leaders.

Chapter 12
Parable of the vineyard, 12.1-12
(Mt 21.33-46; Lk 20.9-19)

Mark. Then he began to speak to them in parables.

Jesus. "A man planted a vineyard, put a fence around it, dug a pit for the wine press, and built a watchtower; then he leased it to tenants and went to another country. [2]When the season came, he sent a slave to the tenants to collect from them his share of the produce of the vineyard. [3] But they seized him, and beat him, and sent him away empty-handed. [4] And again he sent another slave to them; this one they beat over the head and insulted. [5]Then he sent another, and that one they killed. And so it was with many others; some they beat, and others they killed. [6] He had still one other, a beloved son. Finally he sent him to them, saying,

Vineyard owner. 'They will respect my son.'

Jesus. [7] But those tenants said to one another,

Tenants. 'This is the heir; come, let us kill him, and the inheritance will be ours.'

Jesus. [8] So they seized him, killed him, and threw him out of the vineyard. [9] What then will the owner of the vineyard do? He will come and destroy the tenants and give the vineyard to others. [10] Have you not read this scripture:

Temple singer. 'The stone that the builders rejected has become the cornerstone;[a] [11] this was the Lord's doing, and it is amazing in our eyes'?" [b]

Mark. [12] When they realized that he had told this parable against them, they wanted to arrest him, but they feared the crowd. So they left him and went away.

Paying taxes to Caesar, 12.13-17
(Mt 22.15-22; Lk 20.20-26)

Mark. [13] Then they sent to him some Pharisees and some Herodians to trap him in what he said. [14] And they came and said to him,

Pharisees and Herodians. "Teacher, we know that you are sincere, and show deference to no one; for you do not regard people with partiality, but teach the way of God in accordance with truth. Is it lawful to pay taxes to the emperor, or not? [15] Should we pay them, or should we not?"

---

[a] Or *keystone*
[b] Ps 118.22-23

Mark. But knowing their hypocrisy, he said to them,

Jesus. "Why are you putting me to the test? Bring me a denarius and let me see it."

Mark. [16]And they brought one. Then he said to them,

Jesus. "Whose head is this, and whose title?"

Mark. They answered,

Pharisees and Herodians. "The emperor's."

Mark. [17]Jesus said to them,

Jesus. "Give to the emperor the things that are the emperor's, and to God the things that are God's."

Mark. And they were utterly amazed at him.

Question about the resurrection, 12.18-27
(Mt 22.23-33; Lk 20.27-40)

Mark. [18]Some Sadducees, who say there is no resurrection, came to him and asked him a question, saying,

Sadducees. [19]"Teacher, Moses wrote for us that

Moses. (D)(if a man's brother dies, leaving a wife but no child, the man[c] shall marry the widow and raise up children for his brother. [d])

Sadducees. [20]There were seven brothers; the first married and, when he died, left no children; [21]and the second married the widow[e] and died, leaving no children; and the third likewise; [22]none of the seven

---

[c] Gk *his brother*
[d] Deut 25.5
[e] GK *her*

left children. Last of all the woman herself died. [23] In the resurrection[f] whose wife will she be? For the seven had married her."

Mark. [24]Jesus said to them,

Jesus. "Is not this the reason you are wrong, that you know neither the scriptures nor the power of God? [25] For when they rise from the dead, they neither marry nor are given in marriage, but are like angels in heaven. [26] And as for the dead being raised, have you not read in the book of Moses, in the story about the bush, how God said to him,

God. (E)('I am the God of Abraham, the God of Isaac, and the God of Jacob'? [g])

Jesus. [27] He is God not of the dead, but of the living; you are quite wrong."

The great commandment, 12.28-34
(Mt 22.34-40; Lk 10.25-28)

Mark. [28]One of the scribes came near and heard them disputing with one another, and seeing that he answered them well, he asked him,

Scribe. "Which commandment is the first of all?"

Mark. [29] Jesus answered,

Jesus. "The first is,

Moses. (D)('Hear, O Israel: the Lord our God, the Lord is one; [30]you shall love the Lord your God with all your heart, and with all your soul, and with all your mind, and with all your strength.' [h])

---

[f] Other ancient authorities add *when they rise*
[g] Ex 3.6
[h] Deut 6.4-5

Jesus. [31]The second is this,

Moses: (P)('You shall love your neighbor as yourself.' [i])

Jesus. There is no other commandment greater than these."

Mark. [32]Then the scribe said to him,

Scribe. "You are right, Teacher; you have truly said that

Moses.(D)('he is one, and besides him there is no other'; [j])

Scribe. [33] and

Moses. (D)('to love him with all the heart, and with all the understanding, and with all the strength,' [k])

Scribe. and

Moses. (D)('to love one's neighbor as oneself,' [l])

Scribe. —this is much more important than all whole burnt offerings and sacrifices." [m]

Mark. [34]When Jesus saw that he answered wisely, he said to him,

Jesus. "You are not far from the kingdom of God."

Mark. After that no one dared to ask him any question.

---

[i] Lev 19.18
[j] Deut 6.4
[k] Deut 6.5
[l] Lev 19.18
[m] 1 Sam 15.22; Hos 6.6; Mic 6.6-8

David's son, 12.35-37
(Mt 22.41-46; Lk 20.41-44)

Mark. [35]While Jesus was teaching in the temple, he said,

Jesus. "How can the scribes say that the Messiah[n] is the son of David? [36] David himself, by the Holy Spirit, declared,

David. 'The Lord said to my Lord,

Lord. ' "Sit at my right hand, until I put your enemies under your feet." '[o]

Jesus. [37] David himself calls him Lord; so how can he be his son?' "

Mark. And the large crowd was listening to him with delight.

Sayings on pride and humility, 12.38-40

Mark. [38]As he taught, he said,

Jesus. [Q₂]["Beware of the scribes, who like to walk around in long robes, and to be greeted with respect in the marketplaces, [39] and to have the best seats in the synagogues and places of honor at banquets!] [40]They devour widows' houses and for the sake of appearance say long prayers. They will receive the greater condemnation."

The widow's offering, 12.41-44
(Lk 21.1-4)

Mark. [41] He sat down opposite the treasury, and watched the crowd putting money into the treasury. Many rich people put in large sums.

---

[n] Or *the Christ*
[o] Ps 110.1

127

⁴²A poor widow came and put in two small copper coins, which are worth a penny. ⁴³ Then he called his disciples and said to them,

Jesus. "Truly I tell you, this poor widow has put in more than all those who are contributing to the treasury. ⁴⁴For all of them have contributed out of their abundance; but she out of her poverty has put in everything she had, all she had to live on."

Chapter 12 Notes
Parable of the vineyard, 12.1-12

While it may be possible that the parable was part of one of Jesus' parables, it appeared to reflect the beliefs of the early church. The owner of the vineyard was God; the vineyard was Israel; the tenants were the leaders of Judaism; the slaves (servants) were the OT prophets; the beloved son was Jesus; the murder of the heir was the crucifixion of the Jesus; the destruction of the wicked was the destruction of the temple and the new tenants were to be understood as the apostles and the early church.

1: Matthew (Mt 21.33-46) and Mark had this parable presented to the Sanhedrin delegation while Luke had it addressed to the people (Lk 20.9). The parable in Mark, and later Matthew, was closely modeled from the ancient parable in Isaiah (Isa 5.1-7). *Fence around it* missed the point where "wall that was made from stones gathered from the field" was built to keep the wild beasts out of the *vineyard.* A *wine press* was usually hollowed out of rock, with the grapes being crushed in the upper part and the lower part collected the grape-juice. *A watchtower* was an enclosed structure used to store the new wine, and with a flat roof for watchmen to guard the vineyard and wine against beasts and thieves. Luke adapted his version and added the owner went to another country for a long time, that emphasized the length of time since the covenant God made with Moses (Lk 20.10). This may have reflected conditions regarding absentee ownership in Israel, or that God was not present to help the people. **2-5:** The landowner sent several slaves that tried to *collect* from *the tenants* the master's share *of the produce of the vineyard,* usually a quarter or a half of the amount, paid annually. The tenants *beat one, killed another and so it was with many others.* **6-8:** The introduction of *his son,* identified as the *"beloved son"* in Mark and Luke, took what might have been a real situation and made it an allegory. Luke said, "perhaps they will respect him" while Matthew and Mark were more positive, *"they will respect my son."* The foolish tenants thought if *they kill the heir,* the landowner would abandon the vineyard and it would be theirs. Matthew and Luke had the son thrown "out of the vineyard", implying rejection and "killed" (Lk 20.15), while Mark reversed the order (v 8). This may correspond to the Christian tradition that Jesus was crucified "outside the gate." **9:** Roman law did not permit a Jewish master to take matters into his own hands and kill the tenants, but the prophets had repeatedly predicted the destruction of the sinful nation. Matthew and Luke's readers may have thought of the destruction of Jerusalem in 70 CE. Both the Jewish people and the early Christians interpreted this quote from Psalms (Ps 118.22-23) to be messianic (Acts 4.11; 1 Peter 2.4-7). Matthew (Mt 21.43) was the only one to imply that the vineyard would be taken away from Israel and given to a people that produced the fruits of the kingdom, probably meaning the apostles and the church were now the true Israel. Luke added the protest, "Heaven forbid" by Jesus' listeners (Lk 20.16).

12: They wanted to arrest him was an editorial note, but Matthew (Mt 21.45-46) added the reason the chief priests and Pharisees feared the crowd, because the crowd regarded Jesus as a prophet.

Paying taxes to Caesar, 12.13-17

13: (*Egerton Papyrus* 2), "And coming to Jesus to test him, they said, 'Teacher Jesus, we know that you are from God, for what you do testifies to you beyond all the prophets. Tell us, then, is it lawful to give to kings what pertains to their rule? Shall we pay them or not?' And Jesus, knowing their thoughts and being moved with indignation, said to them, 'Why do you call me teacher with your mouth and do not hear what I say? Well did Isaiah prophecy of you, when he said: 'This people honors me with their lips, but their heart is far from me; in vain do they worship me, teaching as doctrines the precepts of human beings.'" **14:** *Herodians* were apparently a group supporting the royal family. Nothing definite was known about them, but probably their interests were secular. The Pharisees sought allies wherever they might be found (Mk 3.6; 8.15; 12.13). In asking Jesus for a pronouncement affecting all Jews, his enemies thought to bring him into conflict with sectarian views. **15-16:** The Romans collected an unpopular annual poll *tax* from every adult male in Judea over the age of fourteen, and all females over twelve, up to the age of sixty-five. This tax was interpreted as a mark of Jewish subjection to a foreign power. The question from the Pharisees and Herodians was carefully presented. If Jesus approved paying taxes, he would offend the nationalistic parties, and if he disapproved payment, he could be reported as disloyal to the empire (Acts 5.37). **16:** *The coin* minted by the Romans with the likeness of the *emperor* was worth about twenty cents. Jewish coins had emblems of olive branches and palms as the Jewish law prohibited the use of images. If coins bearing Caesar's image were circulated, they belonged to the emperor Tiberius, even if the image was his or his predecessor, Augustus, and he had a right to demand them. At the same time, there were duties and debts that were owed to God (Rom 13.7; 1 Pet 2.17). *Gospel of Thomas*, Logion 100, "They showed Jesus a gold (coin) and said to him, 'Caesar's officers demand taxes from us.' Jesus said to them, 'Give to Caesar what belongs to Caesar, give to God what belongs to God, and give to me what is mine.'"

Question about the resurrection, 12.18-27

The Sadducees failed to see God's purpose and did not trust his *power.* The idea here was that those who were related to God in faith had life even though physically dead; resurrection was the divine act by which they would achieve the fullness of life intended in creation and lost through sin and death (see Lk 20.34-36).

18: *The Sadducees* accepted only the written tradition as authorative. Because the belief in a life to come, based on a physical resurrection, emerged after the Pentateuch (first five books of the OT) was compiled and was not evident in it, they declared *there is no resurrection* (Acts 4.1-2; 23.6-10). **19-23:** This was an effort to show that Moses could not have contemplated any resurrection. The reference to the "levirate" marriage law in Deuteronomy (Deut 25.5-6) and Genesis (Gen 38.8) was an ancient Hebrew idea associated with ancestor worship. It was the duty of the brother to have a male descendant for his deceased brother and perpetuate his name and inheritance. By the time of Jesus, this law was in question and was probably obsolete. The case presented by the Sadducees was more about the controversy over the resurrection.

26: All three of the evangelists make the same point, but in somewhat different language; human relationships in the home did not exist in the same way beyond death. Jesus distinguished two ages and kinds of existence. Mortals were part of this age by the fact of physical birth, and of the age to come by resurrection. Marriage was necessary to continue the race, but this disappeared when men and women became like angels and "cannot die anymore" (Lk 20.36). **26-27:** Mark and Luke said, *"In the story about the bush"* (Ex 3.2-6), it would have been nonsense for Moses to speak of the Lord as the God of the patriarchs, if they had only lived and died long ago. To him all of them were alive (Mt 22.32-23; Lk 20.37-40). Interesting parallels were in Fourth Maccabees (4 Macc 7.19; 16.25), written during the same period as Matthew and Luke.

The great commandment, 12.28-34

28-34: Matthew and Luke used the term "lawyer" in place of Mark's *"scribe"* to identify someone who was educated in the religious law. In Mark, the scribe asked about the greatest commandment, and Luke substituted it with one that would have appealed more to the

Gentiles, "what must I do to inherit eternal life?" In Luke, the lawyer combined the Shema in Deuteronomy (Deut 6.4-5) and Leviticus (Lev 19.18), while in Matthew and Mark Jesus made the connection between these OT texts. Jesus stressed that acts of love were the final requirement of the law. Paul quoted this passage in Galatians (Gal 3.12). *Gospel of Thomas,* Logion 25, "Jesus said, 'Love your brother or sister as your soul, and guard them as the apple of your eye.'"

David's son, 12.35-37

35-37: These verses rejected that the Messiah must be "David's son" and suggested that he should be described as *Lord.* All three of the Synoptic Gospel writers had Jesus asking *them,* meaning the *Pharisees,* if the Messiah was David's son? Jesus quoted the first verse of Psalm 110, regarded as a royal psalm. Much was lost from the various translations, because in the OT when the word "LORD" (*see* LORD) was used in reference to God it was capitalized as "LORD" rather than *"Lord"* that was in reference to a king or the Messiah. Therefore, the first LORD referred to God, the second *Lord* was taken to refer to the Messiah. This quote from Psalm 110.1, ascribed to David long before the NT, proclaimed the words that the king (*my lord*) was invited by Israel's God (the LORD) to ascend the throne. The early church interpreted this as prophetic of the ascension in Acts (Acts 2.34-35) and Christ's work as high priest in Hebrews (Heb 1.13 and 10.12-13). Jesus used the opening words of the Psalm to question how the Messiah could be David's descendant, if David called him *Lord.* This did not deny that Jesus was a descendant of David, only that for Jesus the title *"son of David,"* with its political overtones did not do justice to his mission.

Sayings on pride and humility, 12.38-40

38-40: Jesus directed his teaching about the scribes and Pharisees *to the crowds and to his disciples.* While Jesus clashed with the scribes and Pharisees there were times when he was in agreement with them (22.15-33), but after the destruction of the temple in 70 CE, they were the only important influence in Judaism and were in bitter conflict with the early church. Rabbi was a title of respect used by disciples in addressing their elders. This title was commonly used after the destruction of the temple in 70 CE (Mt 23.6-8; Lk 11.43; 14.7-11; 20.46; Jas 3.1).

The widow's offering, 12.41-44

41-44: *The treasury* here referred to a container shaped like an inverted trumpet for protection against theft. There were thirteen of these in the temple court, each labeled telling the purpose for which the money would be used. In John (Jn 8.20), the treasury was a room in the temple. **42:** *Copper coin* (lepton) was of little monetary value, but of great spiritual significance because of its cost to this giver.

Chapter 12 Study Guide

1. Why did Jesus tell the parable of the Vineyard?
2. What is a Christian's position on paying taxes?
3. What does Jesus teach about family relationships in heaven?
4. What does the great commandment mean to you?
5. What does the story of the widow's gift mean to you?

Chapter 13
Destruction of Jerusalem foretold, 13.1 b-2
(Mt 24.1-3; Lk 21.5-7)

Mark. As he came out of the temple, one of his disciples said to him,

Disciple. "Look, Teacher, what large stones and what large buildings!"

Mark. Then Jesus asked him,

Jesus. [2] "Do you see these great buildings? Not one stone will be left here upon another; all will be thrown down."

On the end of the age, 13.3-37
(Mt 24.4-36; Lk 21.8-36)

Mark. [3]When he was sitting on the Mount of Olives opposite the temple, Peter, James, John, and Andrew asked him privately,

Peter, James, John and Andrew. [4] "Tell us, when will this be, and what will be the sign that all these things are about to be accomplished?"

Mark. [5] Then Jesus began to say to them,

Jesus. "Beware that no one leads you astray. [6]Many will come in my name and say,

Messiah. (false) 'I am he!'[a]

Jesus. and they will lead many astray. [7]When you hear of wars and rumors of wars, do not be alarmed; this must take place, but the end is still to come. [8]For nation will rise against nation, and kingdom against kingdom; there will be earthquakes in various places; there will be famines. This is but the beginning of the birth pangs.
    [Q₂][[9] "As for yourselves, beware; for they will hand you over to councils; and you will be beaten in synagogues; and you will stand before governors and kings because of me, as a testimony to them. [10]And the good news[b] must first be proclaimed to all nations. [11]When they bring you to trial and hand you over, do not worry beforehand about what you are to say; but say whatever is given you at that time, for it is not you who speak, but the Holy Spirit. [12]Brother will betray brother to death, and a father his child, and children will rise against parents and have them put to death;] [13] and you will be hated by all

---

[a] Gk *I am*
[b] Gk *gospel*

because of my name. But the one who endures to the end will be saved.

[14] "But when you see the desolating sacrilege set up where it ought not to be

Mark. (let the reader understand),

Jesus. then those in Judea must flee to the mountains; [15] the one on the housetop must not go down or enter the house to take anything away; [Q₂][[16] the one in the field must not turn back to get a coat.] [17] Woe to those who are pregnant and to those who are nursing infants in those days! [18] Pray that it may not be in winter. [19] For in those days there will be suffering, such as has not been from the beginning of the creation that God created until now, no, and never will be. [20]And if the Lord had not cut short those days, no one would be saved; but for the sake of the elect, whom he chose, he has cut short those days. [Q₂][[21] And if anyone says to you at that time,

Messiah. (false) 'Look! Here is the Messiah!'ᶜ

Jesus. or

Messiah. (false) 'Look! There he is!'

Jesus. —do not believe it.] [22] False messiahsᵈ and false prophets will appear and produce signs and omens, to lead astray, if possible, the elect. [23]But be alert; I have already told you everything.

[24] "But in those days, after that suffering, the sun will be darkened, and the moon will not give its light, [25] and the stars will be falling from heaven, and the powers in the heavens will be shaken.

[26] Then they will see 'the Son of Man coming in clouds' with great power and glory. [27]Then he will send out the angels, and gather

---

ᶜ Or *the Christ*
ᵈ Or *christs*

his elect from the four winds, from the ends of the earth to the ends of heaven.

[28] "From the fig tree learn its lesson: as soon as its branch becomes tender and puts forth its leaves, you know that summer is near. [29] So also, when you see these things taking place, you know that he[e] is near, at the very gates. **[Q₃][**[30] Truly I tell you, this generation will not pass away until all these things have taken place. [31] Heaven and earth will pass away, but my words will not pass away."]

[32] "But about that day or hour no one knows, neither the angels in heaven, nor the Son, but only the Father. [33] Beware, keep alert;[f] for you do not know when the time will come. **[Q₂][**[34] It is like a man going on a journey, when he leaves home and puts his slaves in charge, each with his work, and commands the doorkeeper to be on the watch. [35] Therefore, keep awake—for you do not know when the master of the house will come,] in the evening, or at midnight, or at cockcrow, or at dawn, **[Q₂][**[36] or else he may find you asleep] when he comes suddenly. [37] And what I say to you I say to all: Keep awake."

Chapter 13 Notes
Destruction of the Jerusalem foretold, 13.1-2

Mark's Little Apocalypse (Mk 13.1-37) was originally a Jewish document that had been taken over by early Christian preachers to address the circumstances of the early church. It may have included some genuine sayings of Jesus, but they can no longer be isolated. Some of Matthew and Luke's versions differed from Mark's, because they were written later and the beliefs of the early church were more developed.

1-2: These teachings set down by the Evangelist were placed within the historical events that took place between 30 and 70 CE and they predict what might happen at the end of human history. It remains unclear if Jesus predicted the fate of the Jerusalem before its

---

[e] Or *it*
[f] Other ancient authorities add *and pray*

destruction or if it was an after the fact statement by the early church. The actual destruction of Jerusalem was by fire. **3:** Jesus' public ministry ended as he spoke *privately* with his disciples, who asked for a sign when the end would come. Jesus warned them not to expect the end to happen immediately (Lk 17.20-21; Mt 13.39, 40, 49; 16.27).

On the end of the age, 13.3-37

5: *Leads you astray* stressed how important it was to not be misled by false prophets such as Simon Magus (Acts 8.9-11). **6:** Josephus reported during the Jewish war in 66-70 CE there were many who claimed to be a Messiah (1 Jn 2.18). Luke agreed and added to the warning about false messiahs a sense of urgency with the warning, "the time is near" (Lk 21.8). **7-8:** Wars, famines and earthquakes, along with other kinds of cosmic disorders were part of the rhetoric and predictions about the end of the age (2 Esd 9.3; 13.30-32; Rev 6.1-8), and any attempt to link them to specific events of the period of the early church became a waste of time. If they happened, it did not mean the end of time, only that people believed it to be the coming end. It was expected by some that the Jewish war would usher in the end of the age, but it did not happen (Rev 6.3-8, 12, 17). **8:** *The birth pangs* signaled the imminence of the new age, which was announced at the beginning of Jesus' public ministry as come near (4.17), but was to be realized only after a period of witness to Jesus' message (v 14).

9-13: Persecution, false prophets, and apostasy (falling away) were predicted before the end. **10:** *The good news,* about the kingdom of God, *must be proclaimed to all nations* before the end would come was understood to be prophetic by believers today with a different understanding of our inhabited earth. Because the Roman Empire was made up of many nations, it was commonly referred to as "all the nations." Therefore, this verse could be interpreted to mean that the *good news must first be proclaimed* to Rome, and then the end would come (Rom 10.18). In any case, Jesus' followers were to proclaim the good news of the kingdom throughout the world, and it was difficult to explain why most of the disciples remained in Jerusalem after the resurrection while leaving the mission to the Gentiles and mostly to Paul. **13:** *You will be hated by all because of my name* (Jn 15.18; 16.2). For Luke the purpose for all of persecutions was so it "will give you an opportunity to testify" and the disciples were called upon to make up their minds in advance about what they would do (Lk 21.13-14). *But the one who endures to the end* during this trying period *will be saved.*

14-16: *Desolating sacrilege set up where it ought not to be* referred to the establishment of a pagan altar in the temple (Dan 9.27; 11.31; 12.11). The prophecy from Daniel was reinterpreted and applied to the Romans Emperor Caligula (37-41 CE) who wanted to set up his image in the temple. Or it may have been regarding the erection of Titus' statue on the site of the destroyed temple in 70 CE (Mk 13.14). Luke interpreted the expression to mean "When you see Jerusalem surrounded by armies, then you will know that its desolation has come near" (Lk 21.20), revealing some knowledge of the events in Jerusalem just before the siege. The Christian community in Jerusalem withdrew to Pella in Perea in response to the pending disaster. However, the Jewish people came to the city, because they did not believe the temple and the Holy City would be destroyed. According to Roman figures, ninety seven thousand were taken prisoner and one million Jewish people were slain during this war. *Flee to the mountains* because the hill country in Judea had many caves and hiding places. *On the housetop* was regarding the flat roofs where people sat and rested. They were warned not to go into *the house* for any possessions but to flee. Nor should a field laborer attempt to retrieve any property. **17:** *Pregnant women and* mothers with *nursing infants* would not be able to leave fast enough to escape danger. **19:** The mentioning of *winter* was a reference to a time of cold weather. *Gospel of Thomas,* Logion 113, "Jesus' disciples asked him, 'When will the kingdom come?' Jesus said, 'It will not come by waiting for it. People will not say, 'Here it is,' or 'There it is,' but the kingdom of the Father is spread upon the earth and people do not see it.'" **22:** The *signs and omens* were regarding the acts of false prophets (Deut 13.1-5). **24:** The language here was drawn from the OT; God's victory over sin was to be established by the Son of Man whom he sent. *The sun will be darkened* reflected a feature in several Jewish descriptions of the end, "For the stars of the heavens and their constellations will not give their light; the sun will be dark at its rising, and the moon will not shed its light" (Isa 13.10; 34.4; Ezek 32.7; Joel 2.10-11; Zeph 1.15; Rev 8.12). **26:** *They will see 'the Son of Man coming in the clouds'* may be in reference to Isaiah (Isa 11.12), "He will raise a signal for the nations" (16.27; Dan 7.13; Rev 1.7).

30-32: When the early church had to adjust its thinking about the indefinite continuance of history, *this generation* was interpreted to mean either "the race of mankind" or "the company of the faithful" (Mt 24.34; Mk 13.30; Lk 21.32). What Jesus meant, however, was uncertain. Luke omitted Mark's declaration about the exact time being known, *"neither the angels in heaven, nor the Son, but only the Father"* (Mt 24.32; Mk 13.32; Acts 1.6-7). But Luke added, "Heaven and earth will pass away, but my words will not pass away", meaning they were true and eternal (Lk 5.18; 16.17; 21.33).

Chapter 13 Study Guide

1. Why did the disciples remain in Jerusalem after the resurrection, if Jesus told them that the good news must be proclaimed to all nations?
2. Why is it that anytime there is a war some expect this is the end of the world?
3. Why was it difficult for the people to understand and accept that Jesus was the Messiah?
4. Do you believe that the Son of Man will return to usher in the Messianic era?
5. What does this section mean to you? Since the day and hour are unknown, except to God, what is expected of his disciples?

Chapter 14
Jesus' death, 14.1-15.47
(Mt 26.1-27.66; Lk 22.1-23.56; Jn 13.1-19.42)

Mark. It was two days before the Passover and the festival of Unleavened Bread. The chief priests and the scribes were looking for a way to arrest Jesus[a] by stealth and kill him; [2] for they said,

Chief priests and Scribes. "Not during the festival, or there may be a riot among the people."

Mark. [3] While he was at Bethany in the house of Simon the leper,[b] as he sat at the table, a woman came with an alabaster jar of very costly ointment of nard, and she broke open the jar and poured the ointment on his head. [4] But some were there who said to one another in anger,

People. "Why was the ointment wasted in this way? [5] For this ointment could have been sold for more than three hundred denarii,[c] and the money given to the poor."

Mark. And they scolded her. [6]But Jesus said,

Jesus. "Let her alone; why do you trouble her? She has performed a good service for me. [7] For you always have the poor with you, and you can show kindness to them whenever you wish; but you will not always have me. [8]She has done what she could; she has anointed my body beforehand for its burial. [9] Truly I tell you, wherever the good news[d] is proclaimed in the whole world, what she has done will be told in remembrance of her."

Mark. [10] Then Judas Iscariot, who was one of the Twelve, went to the chief priests in order to betray him to them. [11] When they heard

---

[a] Gk *him*
[b] The terms *leper* and *leprosy* can refer to several diseases
[c] The denarius was the usual day's wage for a laborer
[d] Or *gospel*

it, they were greatly pleased, and promised to give him money. So he began to look for an opportunity to betray him.

The Last Supper, 14.12-25
(Mt 26.17-19; Lk 22.7-13)

Mark. [12]On the first day of Unleavened Bread, when the Passover lamb is sacrificed, his disciples said to him,

Disciples. "Where do you want us to go and make the preparations for you to eat the Passover?"

Mark. [13]So he sent two of his disciples, saying to them,

Jesus. "Go into the city, and a man carrying a jar of water will meet you; follow him, [14]And wherever he enters, say to the owner of the house,

Disciples. 'The Teacher asks, Where is my guest room where I may eat the Passover with my disciples?'

Jesus. [15]He will show you a large room upstairs, furnished and ready. Make preparations for us there."

Mark. [16]So the disciples set out and went to the city, and found everything as he had told them; and they prepared the Passover meal.
[17]When it was evening, he came with the twelve. [18]And when they had taken their places and were eating, Jesus said,

Jesus. "Truly I tell you, one of you will betray me, one who is eating with me."

Mark. [19]They began to be distressed and to say to him one after another,

Disciples. "Surely, not I?"

Mark. [20] He said to them,

Jesus. "It is one of the twelve, one who is dipping bread[e] into the bowl[f] with me. [21] For the Son of Man goes as it is written of him, but woe to that one by whom the Son of Man is betrayed! It would have been better for that one not to have been born."

Mark. [22]While they were eating, he took a loaf of bread, and after blessing it he broke it, gave it to them, and said,

Jesus. "Take; this is my body."

Mark. [23]Then he took a cup, and after giving thanks he gave it to them, and all of them drank from it. [24] He said to them,

Jesus. "This is my blood of the[g] covenant, which is poured out for many. [25]Truly I tell you, I will never again drink of the fruit of the vine until that day when I drink it new in the kingdom of God."

Gethsemane, 14.26-52

Mark. [26]When they had sung the hymn, they went out to the Mount of Olives. [27] And Jesus said to them,

Jesus. "You will all become deserters; for it is written,

Lord. 'I will strike the shepherd, and the sheep will be scattered.' [h]

Jesus. [28] But after I am raised up, I will go before you to Galilee."

Mark. [29]Peter said to him,

Peter. "Even though all become deserters, I will not."

---

[e] Gk lacks *bread*
[f] Other ancient authorities read *same bowl*
[g] Other ancient authorities add *new*
[h] Zech 13.7

Mark. ³⁰Jesus said to him,

Jesus. "Truly I tell you, this day, this very night, before the cock crows twice, you will deny me three times."

Mark. ³¹But he said vehemently,

Peter. "Even though I must die with you, I will not deny you."

Mark. And all of them said the same.
³² They went to a place called Gethsemane; and he said to his disciples,

Jesus. "Sit here while I pray."

Mark. ³³ He took with him Peter and James and John, and began to be distressed and agitated. ³⁴ And he said to them,

Jesus. "I am deeply grieved, even to death; remain here, and keep awake."

Mark. ³⁵And going a little farther, he threw himself on the ground and prayed that, if it were possible, the hour might pass from him. ³⁶He said,

Jesus. "Abba,ⁱ Father, for you all things are possible; remove this cup from me; yet, not what I want, but what you want."

Mark. ³⁷ He came and found them sleeping; and he said to Peter,

Jesus. "Simon, are you asleep? Could you not keep awake one hour? ³⁸ Keep awake and pray that you may not come into the time of trial;ʲ the spirit indeed is willing, but the flesh is weak."

ⁱ Aramaic for *Father*
ʲ Or *into temptation*

Mark. [39]And again he went away and prayed, saying the same words. [40]And once more he came and found them sleeping, for their eyes were very heavy; and they did not know what to say to him. [41] He came a third time and said to them,

Jesus. "Are you still sleeping and taking your rest? Enough! The hour has come; the Son of Man is betrayed into the hands of sinners. [42] Get up, let us be going. See, my betrayer is at hand."

Mark. [43]Immediately, while he was still speaking, Judas, one of the twelve, arrived; and with him there was a crowd with swords and clubs, from the chief priests, the scribes, and the elders. [44] Now the betrayer had given them a sign, saying,

Judas Iscariot. "The one I will kiss is the man; arrest him and lead him away under guard."

Mark. [45] So when he came, he went up to him at once and said,

Judas Iscariot. "Rabbi!"

Mark. and kissed him. [46]Then they laid hands on him and arrested him. [47] But one of those who stood near drew his sword and struck the slave of the high priest, cutting off his ear. [48]Then Jesus said to them,

Jesus. "Have you come out with swords and clubs to arrest me as though I were a bandit? [49] Day after day I was with you in the temple teaching, and you did not arrest me. But let the scriptures be fulfilled."

Mark. [50] All of them deserted him and fled. [51] A certain young man was following him, wearing nothing but a linen cloth. They caught hold of him, [52] but he left the linen cloth and ran off naked.

Jesus before Caiaphas, 14.53-72

Mark. [53]They took Jesus to the high priest; and all the chief priests, the elders, and the scribes were assembled. [54]Peter had followed him at a distance, right into the courtyard of the high priest; and he was sitting with the guards, warming himself at the fire. [55]Now the chief priests and the whole council were looking for testimony against Jesus to put him to death; but they found none. [56]For many gave false testimony against him, and their testimony did not agree. [57]Some stood up and gave false testimony against him, saying,

Witnesses. (false) [58]"We heard him say,

Jesus. 'I will destroy this temple that is made with hands, and in three days I will build another, not made with hands.'"

Mark. [59]But even on this point their testimony did not agree. [60]Then the high priest stood up before them and asked Jesus,

Caiaphas. "Have you no answer? What is it that they testify against you?"

Mark. [61]But he was silent and did not answer. Again the high priest asked him,

Caiaphas. "Are you the Messiah,[k] the Son of the Blessed One?"

Mark. [62]Jesus said,

Jesus. "I am; and 'you will see the Son of Man seated at the right hand of the Power,' and 'coming with the clouds of heaven.' "

Mark. [63]Then the high priest tore his clothes and said,

---

[k] Or *the Christ*

Caiaphas. "Why do we still need witnesses? [64] You have heard his blasphemy! What is your decision?"

Mark. All of them condemned him as deserving death. [65] Some began to spit on him, to blindfold him, and to strike him, saying to him,

Chief priests, Scribes and Elders. "Prophesy!"

Mark. The guards also took him over and beat him.
[66] While Peter was below in the courtyard, one of the servant-girls of the high priest came by. [67] When she saw Peter warming himself, she stared at him and said,

Servant girl. "You also were with Jesus, the man from Nazareth."

Mark. [68] But he denied it, saying,

Peter. "I do not know or understand what you are talking about."

Mark. And he went out into the forecourt.[l] Then the cock crowed.[m]
[69] And the servant-girl, on seeing him, began again to say to the bystanders,

Servant girl. "This man is one of them."

Mark. [70] But again he denied it. Then after a little while the bystanders again said to Peter,

Bystanders. "Certainly you are one of them; for you are a Galilean."

Mark. [71] But he began to curse, and he swore an oath,

Peter. "I do not know this man you are talking about."

---

[l] Or *gateway*
[m] Other ancient authorities lack *Then the cock crowed*

Mark. ⁷²At that moment the cock crowed for the second time. Then Peter remembered that Jesus had said to him,

Jesus. "Before the cock crows twice, you will deny me three times."

Mark. And he broke down and wept.

Chapter 14 Notes
Jesus' death, 14.1-15.47

While many of the stories about Jesus and his teachings may have been independent accounts that were later compiled into a chronological account, the same was not true of Jesus' arrest and death. Even if the events did not follow the same order, there existed a clear relationship between John's gospel and the Synoptics. In all probability, the passion narrative was the first to be placed in a fixed form and became the foundation for the gospel accounts. While Mark was considered the oldest account of the passion, Matthew and Luke were probably influenced by early customs and traditions. However, there exists little reason to doubt the validity of these events.

1: *The Passover* commemorated the escape from Egypt under Moses (Ex 12.1-20). It was celebrated on the 15th day of Nisan, and the eight-day *festival of the Unleavened Bread* began on the same day (Ex 12.14-20). The Jewish day was from sundown to sundown and the paschal meal took place on the evening of the 14th, with the lambs having been killed in the temple earlier in the afternoon. In two days, the Passover was coming so Mark and Matthew placed the conspiracy against Jesus on Wednesday the 13th (Mk 14.1-2; Lk 22.1-2; Jn 11.47-53). **2:** *Not during the festival, or there might be a riot among the people,* because during the festival Jerusalem would be crowded with pilgrims, many from Galilee, and the nationalistic expectations were high as they remembered Israel's deliverance from Egypt. Therefore, they planned to arrest and kill Jesus on the very night of their revered festival.

3-9: In John's gospel the anointing of Jesus' feet was done by Mary in the house of Lazarus at Bethany six days before the Passover (Jn 12.1-8). Matthew and Mark (Mt 28.6-13) made no connection between this incident and the previous one. There was no reason provided for the anointing, but it was noted that the head, meaning to make him Messiah, not the feet as in Luke (Lk 7.36-50). Was this an anointing similar to the private anointing of Saul (1 Sam 10.1), or Solomon (1 Kings 1.38-39) or Jehu (2 Kings 9.4-10) that might suggest a revolt with Jesus as the leader? If so, Jesus did not accept it as such, but rather it was an anointing for burial. **3:** *Bethany,* about two miles from Jerusalem, was where Jesus spent his last nights before his arrest. The identity of this Simon remained unknown other than he must have been a cured *leper.* If he still had the disease, people would have avoided contact with him. It could have been that he had the disease and was not at home, but others in the family acted as hosts. **4:** Nothing was known about the *woman* or if she was related to Simon (Jn 12.3; Lk 7.37). To sit or to recline were the customary positions around the table except during the celebration of the Passover when all the seder participants would recline, "as a sign of freedom, we lean to the left when we partake of the wine and the symbolic food. In antiquity, slaves ate hurriedly, standing or squatting on the ground, while royalty, nobility and the wealthy dined on couches. Now we are free and we can recline." John reported the house was filled with the fragrance of the perfume and that the objection to the anointing was by Judas (Jn 12.3-5). Mark commented, *"But some were there who said to one another in anger,"* while Matthew had the *disciples* joining in the protest (Mt 26.8-9), "Why this waste?" **5:** Matthew's a large sum of money used to describe the *ointment* was defined by Mark as *"more than three hundred denarii"* or nearly a year's wages for a laborer. **6:** The *good service* meant what was good and fitting under the circumstances of impending death. The same Greek words were translated "good works" in Matthew (Mt 5.16). **7:** *You always have the poor with you, but you will not always have me* was not being indifferent to the needs of the poor, but to rebuke those who criticized the woman's act of devotion and loyalty. **8-9:** The woman's act won higher praise from Jesus than any other mentioned in the NT (Jn 19.40).

10-11: The obvious question remained, why did Judas betray Jesus? It was not known for certain, but the most popular ideas were centered on Judas being disappointed that Jesus would not openly accept the role of a military Messiah against the Romans and he wanted to force him to defend himself and assume that kingly position. Luke added "then Satan entered into Judas" (Mt 26.14-16; Lk 22.3-6). **10:** *One of the twelve;* the words did not so much identify *Judas* as they intensified the horror of the betrayal. Judas made it possible for a change in the priest's plans. **11:** The value of the "thirty pieces of silver" (Mt 26.15) remained uncertain. Matthew's quotation referred to silver shekels; at four denarii to the shekel, this was one hundred and twenty days' wages (Mt 20.2). All of the Synoptic Gospels implied that Judas merely identified Jesus for those the chief priests sent to make the arrest. There was no evidence to support that he gave the Sanhedrin any information about Jesus or that he was a witness against Jesus or even appeared at the trial. *An opportunity to betray him,* but it was not to be on the Feast day (verse 2) unless their plans had changed.

The Last Supper, 14.12-25

12: *The first day of Unleavened Bread* began after 6 p.m. on Nisan 14th. In the later afternoon the Passover lambs were sacrificed at the temple, and *the Passover* meal was eaten after sunset when the Passover day began (Ex 12.18-27; Deut 16.5-8). All of the gospels agreed that Jesus was crucified on Friday. This date became one of dispute as questions were raised about the Jews allowing the trial and crucifixion to take place on such a holy day as the Passover. On the other hand, it was permissible by Jewish law to try and execute someone convicted to be a false prophet on the Feast day. **13:** Mark only identified the disciples' contact as *a man carrying a jar of water,* who must have been a friend, meant little was said about *the owner of the house.* **16:** *They prepared* meant they purchased, slaughtered and roasted the paschal lamb, cleaned the room of leaven, made the unleavened bread, bitter herbs, and wine available (Mt 21.6; Deut 16.5-8).

17: The tractate *Pesahim* in the *Mishnah* conveyed the main features of the Passover celebration as it had been observed from Jesus' time until today. In addition to the roast lamb, the meal included unleavened bread, bitter herbs, a sauce known as haroseth, a hard-boiled egg, and at least four cups of wine. *And when they had taken their places* probably with Jesus as the father of the family to preside over the meal. The ritual involved blessings over the various elements of the meal, the wine and bread, giving explanations concerning the ritual, and singing of a song of praises for God delivering his people out of Egypt. The only other Jewish meal that could be compared with the Last Supper was the cult meal of the Essenes (1QSa 2.17-22) which was reserved for only those men who belonged in the inner circle (Mt 26.20-25; Lk 22.14, 21-23; Jn 13.21-30). There exists no evidence that Jesus was influenced by the Essenes, but both the Essenes cult meal and the Last Supper reflected Jewish religious practices. **21:** *One of you will betray me* does not require us to believe that Jesus used any supernatural knowledge, because he could have just observed the behavior and attitude of Judas. **19:** *Surely not I?* The response to the question by the disciples, *one after another,* may suggest that each of the disciples thought he was capable of the act of betrayal. **20:** *It is one of the twelve, one who is dipping bread into the bowl with me* did not identify Judas but merely that the betrayer was present within this close group. **21:** *As it is written,* but Jesus did not indicate where it was written and this verse may have been expressing later thoughts by the church (Ps 41.9; Lk 24.25; 1 Cor 15.3; Acts 17.2-3; Mt 18.7). The disciples addressed Jesus as Lord while Judas calls him *Rabbi* (Mt 26.25). Did Matthew hint that Judas' loyalty was beginning to recede?

22-30: These verses seemed to reflect the order of the earliest tradition (Mk 14.22-25; Lk 22.15-20; 22.17; 1 Cor 10.16; 11.23-26; Mt 14.19; 15.36) where the bread was broken first and then the cup was passed. **22:** *The bread* and after *blessing it he broke it* and *gave it to* the disciples, asking them to receive from him and eat this symbol of his broken *body.* **23:** The cup may have been the last of the four cups, the *cup* of Elijah, and *after giving thanks,* and passing it, *and all of them drank from it. Didache* 9.1-5, [1]Concerning the Eucharist, celebrate it in this way: [2]First, concerning the cup: "We give thanks to you, our Father, for the Holy Vine of David your child, which you made known to us through Jesus your child; to you be glory forever. [3]And concerning the broken bread; "We give thanks to you, our Father, for the life and knowledge which you have made known to us through Jesus your child; to you be glory forever. [4]As this broken bread was scattered upon the mountains, but was brought together and became one, so let your church be gathered together from the ends of the earth into your kingdom, for yours is the glory and the power, through Jesus Christ, forever." [5]But let none eat or drink of your Eucharist except those who have been baptized in the Lord's name. For concerning this also the Lord said, "Give not what is holy to the dogs." **24:** The word "new" was added by some ancient authorities making it the blood of the new covenant (Heb 9.20; Mt 20.28; Mk 1.4; Ex 24.6-8; Jer 31.31-34; Mk 14.24). It may not have been in the original text but the idea was presented that God was making a new covenant with his people by the death of Christ. *Poured out for many* that was "a ransom for many" (Mt 20.28). The words "for the forgiveness of sins" were added by Matthew and not present in any of the other accounts. Whether Jesus clearly said at the Last Supper that his death provided forgiveness of sins, he implied it and the disciples understood him to mean that and it was therefore taught as such from the early days of the church. **25:** The Last Supper was not only his farewell meal with the disciples, it was a promise that the Father's kingdom would be established and all of God's people would be united in that messianic banquet (Mt 14.13-21).

Gethsemane, 14.26-31

26: *The hymn* would have been Psalms 115-118, the second part of the Hallel Psalms. *Went out to the Mount of Olives,* which was on the east of Jerusalem. According to the Passover regulation, after the Passover had been eaten within the walls of Jerusalem, the rest of the night was to be spent inside a larger area of Jerusalem, while Bethany was outside this prescribed area, Gethsemane on *the Mount of Olives* was included in it. **27:** On the way to Gethsemane Jesus told the disciples *you will all become deserters* and prepared for Peter's denial (Zech 13.7; Jn 16.32). **28:** *But after I am raised up, I will go ahead of you to Galilee* was omitted from the third century *Fayyum fragment*, "while leading them out Jesus said, 'This night you will all fall away, as it is written, 'I will strike the shepherd, and the sheep will be scattered." When Peter said, "Even though all, not I," Jesus answered, "before the cock crows twice, you will this day deny me three times.'" **30:** *Before the cock crows* was during the third watch before dawn.

32-42: *Gethsemane* meant "olive press" or "olive grove" which was near the Kidron Valley where there were some very old olive trees. Jesus left all but three disciples at the edge of the grove, and he was *deeply grieved, even to death.* **34:** The gospel writers did not usually try to describe Jesus' emotions, but here they revealed some strong feelings at the prospect of torture, rejection, and *death* (Mt 26.38; Lk 22.40-46; Jn 12.27; Heb 5.7-8; Ps 42.6). **35:** Some question what Jesus prayed since he was alone. Matthew and Luke did not put a lot of distance between Jesus and the three disciples, and they could have heard, if they were awake. Mark gave the Aramaic word Jesus used, *"Abba, Father"* asking if God's plan could be realized and his own work finished without suffering death (Ezek 23.31-34; Jn 18.11; Mt 22.20). Jesus did not desire death but accepted God's will even including death. *Cup* implied the cup of suffering (Mt 20.22). It was possible that Jesus at Gethsemane faced the same temptations he encountered in the wilderness, where again he embraced God's will in contrast to self-interests. Luke reported that "an angel from heaven appeared to him and gave him strength as in the wilderness" (Mt 4.11; Mk 1.13). **37-38:** The disciples were warned to stay awake and pray twice in Luke, but three times in Matthew and Mark. These warnings may have been to watch for those that might have approached Jesus, but more likely it was to give support to Jesus in a *time of trial,* when one's best intentions may have given way. Matthew provided the words that Jesus prayed again, "My Father, if this cannot pass unless I drink it, your will be done" (Mt 26.39), then for the third time he agreed with Mark's words, "and prayed, *saying the same words."* **41:** *The hour* of Jesus' arrest, trial and crucifixion *has come* (Jn 12.23; 13.1; 17.1). **42:** Jesus must have seen Judas and the entire party with him, but in sorrow and disappointment he only spoke of Judas, *my betrayer is at hand.*

44: *Now the betrayer had given them a sign* only underscored the tragedy of being betrayed by a chosen follower of Jesus. *A crowd with swords and clubs* as this crowd from the *chief priests, the scribes and elders* evidently expected to encounter considerable resistance by Jesus and his followers. John identified those making the arrest as both Roman soldiers and the Jewish temple police (Jn 18.3). **44:** *The one I will kiss is the man* was to make sure that they arrested the right individual. The Synoptic Gospels did not report Judas' movements on this night (cf Jn 13.30; 18.3). **47:** *One* of Jesus disciples, identified in John as Peter and the slave as Malchus (Jn 18.10-11) *struck the slave of the high priest, cutting off his ear.* Luke said it was the "right ear" and that Jesus touched the ear and healed him, said "No more of this," as fighting to defend Jesus would be self-defeating (Lk 22.50). Verses 52-54 are only found in Matthew (Gen 9.6; Rev 13.10). Twelve legions would be seventy-two thousand angels. **49:** *Day after day* seemed to support that Jesus taught in Jerusalem for a longer period than was presented in the Synoptic Gospels (see notes on Mt 21; Lk 19.47; Jn 18.19-21). *But let the scriptures be fulfilled* seemed to mean he would be deserted by all his followers. Mark added the account of a youth that ran off naked after they caught his linen cloth. Many identified this youth as Mark who added his own signature to the event. Others suggested it connected with the OT (Am 2.16) and that naked did not mean without any clothing, but only wearing an undergarment or tunic (Jn 21.7). Matthew closed this section with, "then all the disciples deserted him and fled," but at least Peter must not have gone too far, because he followed at a distance to the courtyard of the high priest (Mt 26.58).

Jesus before Caiaphas, 14.53-72

53: The Sanhedrin (Jn 11.47) (*see* Sanhedrin) was the Jewish supreme court consisting of seventy priests, scribes and elders, presided over by *the high priest.* While the Sanhedrin could condemn no one to death at night, this was not a formal trial, but an attempt to find a serious charge that would enable them to put him to death. **54:** Peter was often considered weak, but he had the courage to *follow at a distance, right into the courtyard of the high priest,* even to the point of sitting *with the guards* to observe what would happen. **55-58:** At least two witnesses who agreed were required by Numbers (Num 35.30) and Deuteronomy (Deut 19.15) (cf Mt 18.16) *to put* Jesus *to death. But they found none.* **58:** Jesus may have said that the temple would be destroyed, but not that he would destroy it and rebuild it in three days (Mt 24.2; 27.40; Acts 6.14; Jn 2.19). **59-60:** Jesus was invited by *the high priest* to defend himself, concerning the charge of destroying the temple. **61:** When Jesus remained silent, concerning the false charge, *the high priest* asked him if he was *the Messiah, the Son of the Blessed One* (Jn 18.33). **62:** Jesus responded to this question with *"I am."* Then without either using the title Messiah or the Son of God, Jesus refers to *the Son of Man seated at the right hand of Power* next to God, as *coming* to establish God's kingdom (Mt 16.28; Dan 7.13; Ps 110.1). **63-64:** *The high priest tore his clothes,* but he was pleased because Jesus' response was considered *blasphemy.* In the rabbinic tradition, the only blasphemy punishable by death was that of cursing God by name pronouncing the name of "YHVH" (Num 14.6; Acts 14.14; Lev 24.16). Here the only thing that Jesus said that could be considered blasphemy was in Mark when he said, *"I am."* The rest of the Sanhedrin agreed with the high priest, *as deserving death,* but they did not have the legal right to carry out the sentence. **65:** Expressing their hate and contempt the Sanhedrin mocked Jesus, *some* spit *in his face, blindfold him,* slapped him and asked him to *prophesy.*

66-71: Peter spoke with a Galilean accent setting him apart from the Judeans (Acts 2.7). The oddities of the Galilean speech patterns and dress were ridiculed in the Talmud. *This man is one of them* may have been regarding Judas or another disciple (Jn 18.15)? Or was it challenging Peter's courage to be present at the courtyard? With repeated curses and oaths, Peter denied that he even knew Jesus. **72:** *The cock crows* and Peter was reminded of what Jesus told him and his inability to remain faithful in the face of adversity (cf v 34), and he *broke down and wept.*

Chapter 14 Study Guide

1. What is your understanding of the festival of the Unleavened Bread and the Passover?
2. Why do you think the woman anointed Jesus at the house of Simon the leper?
3. Why did Judas betray Jesus to the chief priests?
4. What is the significance of the bread and the cup for you?
5. Why was there such a large group present to arrest Jesus?

Chapter 15
Jesus before Pilate, 15.1-15

Mark. As soon as it was morning, the chief priests held a consultation with the elders and scribes and the whole council. They bound Jesus, led him away, and handed him over to Pilate. ² Pilate asked him,

Pilate. "Are you the King of the Jews?"

Mark. He answered him,

Jesus. "You say so."

Mark. ³ Then the chief priests accused him of many things. ⁴ Pilate asked him again,

Pilate. "Have you no answer? See how many charges they bring against you."

Mark. [5] But Jesus made no further reply, so that Pilate was amazed.
[6] Now at the festival he used to release a prisoner for them, anyone for whom they asked. [7] Now a man called Barabbas was in prison with the rebels who had committed murder during the insurrection. [8] So the crowd came and began to ask Pilate to do for them according to his custom. [9] Then he answered them,

Pilate. "Do you want me to release for you the King of the Jews?"

Mark. [10] For he realized that it was out of jealousy that the chief priests had handed him over. [11] But the chief priests stirred up the crowd to have him release Barabbas for them instead. [12] Pilate spoke to them again,

Pilate. "Then what do you wish me to do[a] with the man you call[b] the King of the Jews?"

Mark. [13] They shouted back,

Crowd. "Crucify him!"

Pilate. [14] "Why, what evil has he done?"

Mark. But they shouted all the more,

Crowd. "Crucify him!"

Mark. [15] So Pilate, wishing to satisfy the crowd, released Barabbas for them; and after flogging Jesus, he handed him over to be crucified.

---

[a] Other ancient authorities read *what should I do*
[b] Other ancient authorities lack *the man you call*

The crucifixion, 15.16-47

Mark. [16]Then the soldiers led him into the courtyard of the palace (that is, the governor's headquarters[c]); and they called together the whole cohort. [17] And they clothed him in a purple cloak; and after twisting some thorns into a crown, they put it on him. [18] And they began saluting him,

Soldiers. "Hail, King of the Jews!"

Mark. [19]They struck his head with a reed, spat upon him, and knelt down in homage to him. [20] After mocking him, they stripped him of the purple cloak and put his own clothes on him. Then they led him out to crucify him.

[21] They compelled a passer-by, who was coming in from the country, to carry his cross; it was Simon of Cyrene, the father of Alexander and Rufus. [22] Then they brought Jesus[d] to the place called Golgotha (which means the place of a skull). [23]And they offered him wine mixed with myrrh; but he did not take it. [24] And they crucified him, and divided his clothes among them, casting lots to decide what each should take.

[25] It was nine o'clock in the morning when they crucified him. [26] The inscription of the charge against him read,

Charge against Jesus. "The King of the Jews."

Mark. [27] And with him they crucified two bandits, one on his right and one on his left.[e] [29] Those who passed by derided[f] him, shaking their heads and saying,

---

c   Gk *the praetorium*
d   Gk *him*
e   Other ancient authorities add verse 28, *And the scripture was fulfilled that says, "And he was counted among the lawless."*
f   Or *blasphemed*

Bystanders. "Aha! You who would destroy the temple and build it in three days, ³⁰ save yourself, and come down from the cross!"

Mark. ³¹In the same way the chief priests, along with the scribes, were also mocking him among themselves and saying,

Chief priests and Scribes. "He saved others; he cannot save himself. ³² Let the Messiah,ᵍ the King of Israel, come down from the cross now, so that we may see and believe."

Mark. Those who were crucified with him also taunted him.
 ³³ When it was noon, darkness came over the whole landʰ until three in the afternoon. ³⁴At three o'clock Jesus cried out with a loud voice,

Jesus. "Eloi, Eloi, lema sabachthani?"

Mark. which means,

Jesus. "My God, my God, why have you forsaken me?"ⁱ

Mark. ³⁵When some of the bystanders heard it, they said,

Bystanders. "Listen, he is calling for Elijah."

Mark. ³⁶And someone ran, filled a sponge with sour wine, put it on a stick, and gave it to him to drink, saying,

Bystanders. "Wait, let us see whether Elijah will come to take him down."

Mark. ³⁷Then Jesus gave a loud cry and breathed his last. ³⁸ And the curtain of the temple was torn in two, from top to bottom. ³⁹Now

---

ᵍ Or *the Christ*
ʰ Or *earth*
ⁱ Other ancient authorities read *made me a reproach*; Ps 22.1

when the centurion, who stood facing him, saw that in this way he[j] breathed his last, he said,

Centurion. "Truly this man was God's Son!"[k]

Mark. [40]There were also women looking on from a distance; among them were Mary Magdalene, and Mary the mother of James the younger and of Joses, and Salome. [41] These used to follow him and provided for him when he was in Galilee; and there were many other women who had come up with him to Jerusalem.

[42] When evening had come, and since it was the day of Preparation, that is, the day before the sabbath, [43] Joseph of Arimathea, a respected member of the council, who was also himself waiting expectantly for the kingdom of God, went boldly to Pilate and asked for the body of Jesus. [44] Then Pilate wondered if he were already dead; and summoning the centurion, he asked him whether he had been dead for some time. [45] When he learned from the centurion that he was dead, he granted the body to Joseph. [46]Then Joseph[l] bought a linen cloth, and taking down the body,[m] wrapped it in the linen cloth, and laid it in a tomb that had been hewn out of the rock. He then rolled a stone against the door of the tomb. [47] Mary Magdalene and Mary the mother of Joses saw where the body[n] was laid.

Chapter 15 Notes
Jesus before Pilate, 15.1-15

1-2: Matthew and Mark reported of a hearing at night by the Sanhedrin and the high priest to establish a charge and to find the proper witnesses (Mt 27.1; Lk 23.1; Jn 18.28-32). Jewish law required that the Sanhedrin take formal action by daylight. Apparently,

---

[j] Other ancient authorities add *cried out and*
[k] Or *a son of God*
[l] Gk *he*
[m] Gk *it*
[n] Gk *it*

Matthew (Mt 26.57-68) described a pre-dawn hearing. Pilate was appointed Procurator of the Providence of Judea by Tiberius in 26 CE and was replaced in 36 CE. Pilate was not always on the best terms with the Jewish people, because he brought troops into Jerusalem without removing their insignia that bore the emperor's picture. He also once used temple funds to construct an aqueduct. **11-14:** Compare these verses with Matthew (Mk 15.2-5), Luke (Lk 23.2-5), and John (Jn 18.29-19.16). **5:** *Pilate was amazed* because most men, guilty or not, would protest of their innocence (Lk 23.9; Mt 26.62; Mk 14.60; 1 Tim 6.13).

6-15: To appease the national enthusiasm of the crowd during a festival, the Romans followed an ancient world custom and permitted the people to choose a prisoner to be released (Mt 27.15-26; Lk 23.18-25; Jn 18.38-40; 19.4-16). *Flogging* with a multi-thronged whip ordinarily preceded execution (Mt 27.26).

The crucifixion, 15.16-47

16: Soldiers of the governor usually accompanied the governor from Caesarea to Jerusalem and assisted in keeping order during the festival. *The governor's headquarters* was the official residence of the governor. *The cohort* at full strength numbered about five thousand men. **17-19:** *A purple cloak* was probably a soldier's purple mantle, the imitation of an imperial robe. *Twisting some thorns into a crown* was similar to the garland awarded to the victor in battle or at the games. It was used here in mockery of a royal crown, and *struck his head with a reed* as to anoint him, but they *spat upon him,* and then *knelt down in* (mock) *homage to him.* **20:** Probably the soldier wanted his purple robe back, since the Roman soldiers had to purchase their own uniforms. So they *stripped him of the purple robe and put his own clothes on him* before they *led him out to crucify him.*

21: John said that Jesus carried his own cross, and this might have been done for a short distance (Jn 19.17). When they came outside the city and met Simon of Cyrene, *they compelled* him *to carry* Jesus' cross, maybe because Jesus was weak from the flogging. Mark identified *Simon of Cyrene as the father of Alexander and Rufus.* It was Roman custom that the condemned individual did not carry the entire cross, but only the cross beam because the upright beam was standing ready to receive it (Mk 15.21; Lk 23.26, 33-43; Jn 19.17-24). **22:** The procession included Jesus, two other prisoners, a centurion, and a few soldiers. *Golgotha* in Aramaic meant *skull* or head and was located outside of the second wall of Jerusalem. **23:** *Wine mixed with myrrh* and possibly with gall was a bitter liquid offered to ease the pain of crucifixion (Ps 49.4-21). It remained unclear if this mixture was the custom, or requested by someone, or was an act of kindness. Matthew said, "When he tasted it," he realized what it was and would not drink it, choosing to endure the pain (Mt 27.34). **24:** *And they crucified him* meant Jesus was probably laid down upon the cross beam, his hands nailed to each end and then the cross beam with Jesus on it was lifted and fixed to the upright beam. Perhaps the feet were then nailed to the upright beam. *And divided his clothes,* as it was the Roman custom. *His clothes* were mainly: a headdress, cloak or outer garment; belt; shoes; tunic or inner garment. Since the soldier had already taken his robe back (v 31), contrary to public belief today it was not there to be won by casting lots. The tunic was seamless like that of the high priest and was symbolic of the controversy over Jesus as the high priest (Jn 19.23; Ps 22.18), and it was of some value. Only Matthew included, that the soldiers "sat down there and kept watch over him," probably to prevent anyone from rescuing him (Mt 27.36).

    26: It was a Roman custom to put a titular around the neck of the criminal indicating the offense. Since the Romans recognized Herod as the ruler, to label Jesus as a pretender and revolutionary served as a warning to the pilgrims from the remote parts of the region. Jesus was crucified on the charge of having claimed to be the Messiah, a king (Jn 19.12-16). **27:** *Two bandits* were identified in a later tradition as Zoatham and Camma. **29:** *Shaking their heads* was an Oriental gesture of scorn as in the Psalms, "All who see me mock at me; they make mouths at me, they shake their heads" (Ps 22.7; 109.25). **30:** The taunts stressed religious aspects of Jesus' works and words. *Israel* (rather than *the Jews,* v 26) referred to the religious community rather than the political state. **31:** *The chief priests, along with the scribes, were also mocking* Jesus, "if he was *the King of Israel,* let him *come down from the cross,* and we will believe in him."

33-38: *Gospel of Peter,* 5.15-20, "Now it was noon, and darkness covered over all Judea, and they were afraid and distressed for fear the sun had set while Jesus was still alive. For it is written for them that the sun should not set upon one put to death. And one of them said, 'Give him gall with vinegar to drink.' And they mixed them and gave it to him. And they fulfilled all things and brought their sins to an end upon their own heads. And many went about with lamps, supposing it was night, and they went to bed. And the Lord cried out, 'My power, my power, you have forsaken me!' and saying this Jesus was taken up. In the same hour the curtain of the temple of Jerusalem was torn in two." **34:** *Eli, lema sabachthani,* was quoted from Psalm (Ps 22.1). **35:** *Some of the bystanders* may have been Jewish individuals who knew about Elijah. *Elijah* (similar in sound to Eli) was expected to usher in the final period (Mal 4.5-6; Mt 27.49). **36:** The motive in offering the *sour wine* may have been to revive him and hence prolong the ordeal (Ps 69.21). **38:** *The curtain of the temple* before the Holy of Holies *was torn in two, from top to bottom.* By his death Jesus opened direct access to God for the people (Heb 9.8; 10.19; Ex 26.31-35; Mt 28.2; Mk 15.38). *Gospel of the Nazaraeans,* (in Jerome, *Letter 120 to Hedibia* and *Commentary on Matthew 27.51*), "...of Zebedee and Salome, and the women who followed Jesus from Galilee seeing Jesus who had been crucified. It was the day of Preparation, that is, the day before the sabbath, a man named Joseph of Erinmathaias, a city of Judea. Being a disciple of Jesus, he was good and righteous, but had been condemned secretly on account of the fear of the Jews, and he looked for the kingdom of God. He had not consented to the purpose..." **39:** The words, *"Truly this man was God's Son"* for the Roman centurion might have implied the son of a pagan god, but for Mark it was an expression of faith that Christians can hear with deep understanding. **40:** *James* was possibly the James of 10.3; Lk 24.10; Acts 1.13.

42-47: Jesus died shortly after 3 p.m. on Friday and the sabbath would begin at sundown, and leaving the body of an executed criminal hang overnight was forbidden (Deut 21.23; Mk 15.42-47; Lk 23.50-56; Jn 19.38-42; Acts 13.29). *Joseph of Arimathea* who lived a little over twenty miles north-west of Jerusalem had moved to Jerusalem and being a rich man purchased his own *tomb which had been hewn out of the rock. Gospel of Peter*, 2.3-5a, "Joseph, the friend of Pilate and of the Lord, was standing there; and knowing that they were about to crucify Jesus, he went to Pilate and asked for the body of the Lord for burial. And Pilate sent word to Herod and asked for the body. And Herod responded, 'Brother Pilate, even if no one asked for the body, we would bury it, since it is almost the sabbath. For it is written in the law, 'Let not the sun set on one who has been put to death.'" *Gospel of Peter,* 6.21-24, "And then they drew out the nails from the hands of the Lord, and laid the body upon the earth. And the whole earth was shaken, and a great fear arose. Then the sun shone and it was found to be the ninth hour. The Jews rejoiced and gave Jesus' body to Joseph, to bury it, because he had seen all the good things that Jesus had done. And Joseph took the body of the Lord, and washed it, and wrapped it in a linen shroud, and brought it to his own tomb, called the garden of Joseph." **43:** Ancient rulers sometimes gave the body of an executed criminal to friends for burial. **46:** Joseph rolled *a stone against the door of the tomb,* perhaps with the help of his servants as there was no hint of any disciples being there (Jn 19.39; Mk 16.3-5; Acts 13.29). **47:** The two Marys were watching and later they could tell of the burial (27.56).

Chapter 15 Study Guide

1. What role did Pilate pay in the trial of Jesus? Could he have done more to stop the crucifixion?
2. Who chose Barabbas over Jesus? Why?
3. What does Jesus being crucified mean to you?
4. Explain the curtain in the temple being torn into, from the top to the bottom?

5. What was the importance of having the women know where the body was laid?

Chapter 16
The first Easter, 16.1-8
(Mt 28.1-10; Lk 24.1-11; Jn 20.1-10)

Mark. When the sabbath was over, Mary Magdalene, and Mary the mother of James, and Salome bought spices, so that they might go and anoint him. [2]And very early on the first day of the week, when the sun had risen, they went to the tomb. [3]They had been saying to one another,

Mary Magdalene, Mary and Salome. "Who will roll away the stone for us from the entrance to the tomb?"

Mark. [4]When they looked up, they saw that the stone, which was very large, had already been rolled back. [5]As they entered the tomb, they saw a young man, dressed in a white robe, sitting on the right side; and they were alarmed. [6]But he said to them,

Man in white robe. "Do not be alarmed; you are looking for Jesus of Nazareth, who was crucified. He has been raised; he is not here. Look, there is the place they laid him. [7]But go, tell his disciples and Peter that he is going ahead of you to Galilee; there you will see him, just as he told you."

Mark. [8]So they went out and fled from the tomb, for terror and amazement had seized them; and they said nothing to anyone, for they were afraid.[a]

---

[a] Some of the most ancient authorities bring the book to a close at the end of verse 8. One authority concludes the book with the shorter ending; others include the shorter ending and then continue with verses 9-20. In most authorities verses 9-20 follow immediately after verse 8, though in some of these authorities the passage is marked as being doubtful.

THE SHORTER ENDING OF MARK

MARK. [[And all that had been commanded them they told briefly to those around Peter. And afterward Jesus himself sent out through them, from east to west, the sacred and imperishable proclamation of eternal salvation.[b]]]

THE LONGER ENDING OF MARK
The traditional close of the Gospel of Mark, 16.9-20
Post-resurrection appearances of Jesus, 16.9-18

MARK. [9] [[Now after he rose early on the first day of the week, he appeared first to Mary Magdalene, from whom he had cast out seven demons. [10] She went out and told those who had been with him, while they were mourning and weeping. [11]But when they heard that he was alive and had been seen by her, they would not believe it.

[12]After this he appeared in another form to two of them, as they were walking into the country. [13]And they went back and told the rest, but they did not believe them.

[14]Later he appeared to the eleven themselves as they were sitting at the table; and he upbraided them for their lack of faith and stubbornness, because they had not believed those who saw him after he had risen.[c] [15] And he said to them,

Jesus. "Go into all the world and proclaim the good news[d] to the whole creation. [16]The one who believes and is baptized will be saved; but the one who does not believe will be condemned. [17] And these signs will accompany those who believe: by using my name they

---

[b] Other ancient authorities add *Amen*

[c] Other ancient authorities add, in whole or in part, *And they excused themselves, saying, "This age of lawlessness and unbelief is under Satan, who does not allow the truth and power of God to prevail over the unclean things of the spirits. Therefore reveal your righteousness now"—thus they spoke to Christ. And Christ replied to them, "The term of years of Satan's power has been fulfilled, but other terrible things draw near. And for those who have sinned I was handed over to death, that they may return to the truth and sin no more, that they may inherit the spiritual and imperishable glory of righteousness that is in heaven."*

[d] Or *gospel*

will cast out demons; they will speak in new tongues; [18] they will pick up snakes in their hands,[e] and if they drink any deadly thing, it will not hurt them; they will lay their hands on the sick, and they will recover."

Jesus' exaltation, 16.19-20

Mark. [19]So then the Lord Jesus, after he had spoken to them, was taken up into heaven and sat down at the right hand of God. [20]And they went out and proclaimed the good news everywhere, while the Lord worked with them and confirmed the message by the signs that accompanied it.[f]]]

Chapter 16 Notes
The first Easter, 16.1-8

Recorded differences in the resurrection help the reader to understand what the early church believed about the event and its importance for the community of faith. The message of Peter and the early church was that Jesus, the Messiah, died on the cross, was buried, and was raised from the grave by God (Acts 2.14-36). Paul wrote, no more than twenty-five years after the resurrection, about the event (1 Cor 15.3-8), and his teaching about it was based upon apostolic doctrine (1 Cor 15.9-11). Yet, the reader remains struck by Paul not referring to the empty tomb in any of his letters, and his own conviction of the resurrection was that a spiritual body was waiting for the soul of man in heaven (1 Cor 15.35-55; 2 Cor 5.1-4).

1-8: However, the empty tomb appealed to Mark who believed it important enough to include in his gospel, even if the details were not clear. *Mary Magdalene, Mary and Salome* had some *spices* to *anoint* the body of Jesus and were concerned as to *who will roll away the stone for us from the entrance to the tomb.* They found the *very*

---

[e] Other ancient authorities lack *in their hands*
[f] Other ancient authorities add *Amen*

large stone *already rolled back* and upon entering the tomb, they were greeted by a young *man, dressed in a white robe.* Luke had two men in dazzling white clothes at the tomb who ask the question, "Why do you look for the living among the dead" (Lk 24.5)? They are told that *Jesus of Nazareth, who was crucified* was not here, *he has been raised.* Mark did not indicate that the *young man* possessed a supernatural element only that he was clothed in a *white robe* and his only function was to proclaim that Jesus *has been raised* and to deliver a message for the *disciples and Peter.* No reason was given for singling out Peter from the rest of the disciples, but the message was that Jesus was *going ahead of you to Galilee* and that they would see him there. Instead of running away, the women were called upon by Luke to "remember how he told you, while he was still in Galilee" (Lk 24.6). **8:** Mark's gospel closed with these words: *So they went out and fled from the tomb, for terror and amazement had seized them; and they said nothing to anyone, for they were afraid.*

The traditional close of the Gospel of Mark, 16.9-20

Nothing is certainly known either about how this gospel originally ended or about the origin of vv 9-20, which, because of the textual evidence and stylistic differences from the rest of the gospel, cannot have been part of the original text of Mark. Certain important witnesses to the text, including some ancient ones, end the gospel with verse 8. Though it is possible that the compiler of the gospel intended this abrupt ending, one can find hints he intended to describe events after the resurrection. For example Mk 14.28 looks forward to an account of at least one experience of the disciples with Jesus in Galilee after the resurrection, while the friendly reference to Peter (16.7) may anticipate the recounting of the otherwise unrecorded moment of reconciliation between Peter and his Lord (cf Lk 24.34; 1 Cor 15.5). If accounts such as these were originally part of Mark's gospel, the loss of them took place very shortly after the gospel was written, under circumstances beyond present knowledge. Many manuscripts, some ancient, end the gospel with vv 9-20, thus showing that from early Christian times these verses have been accepted traditionally and generally as part of the canonical gospel of Mark.

A variety of other manuscripts concluded the gospel with the shorter ending, either alone or followed by verses 9-20, thus indicating that different attempts were made to provide a suitable ending for the Gospel. The longer ending may have been compiled early in the second century as a didactic summary of grounds for the belief in Jesus' resurrection, being appended to the gospel by the middle of the second century. On the Christian belief in continuing unrecorded memories about Jesus in the first century (see Lk 1.1-2; Jn 20.30, 21.25; Acts 20.35; 1 Cor 15.3; also compare Mt 28.20; Jn 16.12-33; Rev 1.12-16; 2.18).

Post-resurrection Appearances of Jesus, 16.9-18

10-11: There was no indication by Mark, in the shorter ending of this gospel that the women, who were gripped with terror and amazement, had done anything but kept these words to themselves because they were afraid. However, in the longer ending of the gospel, Mary Magdalene told *those who had been with him* he was alive and seen by her, but they would not believe it.

14: It is only after Jesus appeared to the *eleven* with a message for them to *"Go into all the world and proclaim the good news to the whole creation..."* that they believed. The matter of Galilee gave rise to many questions. Was Galilee, instead of Jerusalem, to be the center of the messianic kingdom, when the Son of Man would return (parousia)? From the writings, concerning the Son of Man there was evidence it was a prophecy of the northern part of Israel that was non-nationalistic and universal. Mark mentioned Galilee several times in his gospel and assumed it to be the center of Jesus' ministry. The center of Jesus' opposition was not in Galilee but it came from Jerusalem. Yet, later on James resided in Jerusalem and was the leader of the church in Judea. Mark and later Matthew seemed to have the center of the early church in Galilee while Luke and John had the center in Jerusalem. **17-18:** The reality of faith in believers' lives as they responded to the apostolic witness was signified by events that both correspond with biblically recorded happenings in the lives of the apostles and conformed to apostolic statements about the gifts of the Spirit (1 Cor 12.8-11, 28; 14.2-5; Heb 2.3-4): exorcism (Acts 8.6-7; 16.18; 19.11-20), new tongues (Acts 2.4-11; 10.46; 19.6; 1 Cor 12.9; 28; 14.2-33), and healing (Acts 28.8, 1 Cor 12.9; Jas 5.13-16). Instances of picking up a snake and drinking poison, without injury to the believers in either case, lacked NT parallels. However, the former resembled the harmless accidental attack upon Paul in Acts (Acts 28.3-6), and the latter appeared occasionally in Christian literature from the second century onward. *Gospel of Peter,* 12.50-54, 13.55-57, [50]Now early on the Lord's day Mary Magdalene, a disciple of the Lord, who was afraid because of the Jews (for they were inflamed with anger, and the women had not done at the tomb of the Lord the things that women usually do to their loved ones when they die) – [51]Mary took friends with her, and went to the tomb where Jesus was laid. [52]And they feared lest the Jews see them, and they said, "Even if we were not able to weep and lament for Jesus on the day of the crucifixion, yet let us not do so at the tomb. [53]But who will roll away for us the stone that is set against the door of the tomb, that we may enter and sit beside Jesus, and perform our obligations?" [54]For the stone was very large." We fear lest some one see us. But if we cannot, then let us lay beside the door the things which we have brought in remembrance of Jesus, and we will weep and lament until we get home." [13.55]And they went and found the tomb open; and going near, they looked in, and saw there a young man sitting in the middle of the tomb, handsome, and dressed in a brilliant robe. And the angel said to them, [56]"Why have you come? Whom do you seek? Not the one who was crucified, for that one has risen and gone. But if you do not believe it, look in and see the place where the body lay, that it is not here. For Jesus has risen and gone to the place from which Jesus was sent." [57]Then the women were afraid and fled.

Jesus' exaltation, 16.19-20

19: In order to understand the concept of Jesus' exaltation, see Phil 2.9-11; Heb 1.3; for the language *was taken up,* read Acts 1.2,

11, 22; 1 Tim 3.16 (seemingly a Christian hymn); for the image of the *right hand of God,* consider Ps 110.1; Acts 7.55; Heb 1.3.

Chapter 16 Study Guide

1. How do you explain that at times Jesus appeared in the flesh?
2. What was the commission that Jesus presented to the disciples?
3. What is the significance of the resurrection for you?
4. What is your understanding about the message to meet the disciples in Galilee?
5. What does the longer ending add to Mark's gospel?

Sources in Mark

In both the cast and the notes following the Bible in Dialogue text, reference was made to several church fathers, books and manuscripts. Many of the sources, while taken for granted by many biblical scholars remain unknown to those sitting in the pews on Sunday morning, primarily because of a lack of exposure to them. Therefore, it seemed important to provide some historical information about these sources.

Augustine. Augustine born in North Africa in 354, died in August 430. He was chiefly known for his *Confessions, City of God,* commentaries, etc. These works have had a tremendous influence on subsequent theology and writers such as Paul Tillich.

Clement of Alexandria. Clement was the successor of Pantaenus as head of the Alexandrian catechetical school from *ca* 200 until his death about 215. He was also a presbyter in the Alexandrian church. Perhaps not a great theologian, Clement was a Greek puritan who understood philosophy to be a servant of Christianity, having led the Greeks to Christ. Four of his more important surviving works are, the *Exhortation to the Heathen;* the *Protrepticus,* or *Address,* designed to convert pagans; the *Instructor,* the first treatise on Christian conduct; and the *Stromateis,* or *Miscellanies*, which was a scrapbook of many thoughts Clement wished to preserve.

Codex. The Latin term Codex meant a tree-stump that became a slab of wood for writing. It became known as a wax-coated board used for note taking. Eventually the term applied to the flat, rectangular piles of paper, or sometimes parchment, that became a book, rather than a roll or scroll. The codex was used by Christians well before 100 CE.

Codex Bezae. This fifth century Codex, contained most of the Golden Rule and Acts, with a small fragment of Third John, written on vellum in both Greek and Latin. The four hundred and six (406) of the original five hundred thirty-four (534) parchment leaves appeared in Greek on the left face and in Latin or the right face of the Codex. The Bishop of Clermont borrowed the Codex from the Monastery of St. Irenaeus in Lyons to take it to the Council of Trent in 1546. It was returned to Lyons only later to fall into the hands of Theodore de'Bezae, a Geneva scholar and reformer, who presented it to the University of Cambridge in 1581. Since then the Codex has been called by his name, *Codex Bezae.*

Codex Vaticanus. A Greek Codex from the fourth century was called *Codex Vaticanus.* It originally contained both the OT and NT, but Hebrews 9.14-13.25, the Pastoral Epistles, Philemon and the Apocalypse. It was the best Alexandrian text available of the gospels and Acts. It appeared in a 1475 catalog of the Vatican library with no information about its earlier history. For hundreds of years no one outside the Vatican could copy it or even study a section long enough to remember it. Its presence was known in 1553 but no one knew about its contents until one hundred and fifty years later when Napoleon carried the manuscript off to Paris as a victory prize. It was studied in Paris by Hug who revealed its age and importance (1810). In 1815, it was returned to the Vatican with many other treasures taken by Napoleon, only to become inaccessible to scholars once again until 1843, when Tischendorf could view the manuscript for six hours. In 1857 Cardinal Mai published an edition of the work, and in 1866 Tischendorf again could study it for no longer than three hours per day and not to copy any of it. After eight days, he had copied eight pages and his permission was revoked only to be restored later for six more days, enabling him to publish an edition in 1867. Finally, in 1889-1890 a photographic copy of the manuscript was made available to all scholars.

Didache. The *Didache,* otherwise known as the *"Teaching of the Twelve Apostles"* first appeared *ca* 100-110 CE as a brief formulation of the rules of conduct Christians should observe.

Egerton Papyrus 2. The Egerton Papyrus, a group of fragments of an unknown gospel found in Egypt, were sold to the British Museum in 1934. The fragments were dated about the end of the second century CE, but the date of composition was perhaps 50-100 CE. It was one of the oldest known fragments of any gospel, or any codex. It was also called the *Unknown gospel,* since no ancient source referred to it.

Fayum Fragment. This fragment, identified as *Fayum Fragment,* from the third century contained words similar to Mark 14.27-30, except for verse 28. It was discovered by G. Brickell in Vienna in 1885, among the collection of Archduke Rainer. Scholars debated if the fragment came from a text of the gospel or if it was a homiletical paraphrase of Mark 14.27-30.

Gospel according to the Ebionites. This *Gospel according to the Ebionites,* written in Greek during the first half of the second century, may have been an abridged and altered form of the gospel of Matthew. The Ebionites, a Jewish Christian sect, who denied the virgin birth and believed that Jesus' sonship to God rested entirely on the union of the Holy Spirit with Jesus made at his baptism, used this gospel. The seven extant fragments of the work were found in Epiphanius, *Against Heresies* XXX. 13-22.

Gospel according to the Egyptians.– This *Gospel according to the Egyptians,* probably from the first half of the second century, was used by Christians in Egypt perhaps as their only "life of Jesus." Though Gnosticism influenced it, II Clement quoted it. Clement of Alexandria also quoted it (*Miscellanies,* Book III), and not as heresy; but Origen regarded this gospel as heretical. Its view on sexual matters was one of self-denial and self-discipline.

Gospel according to the Hebrews. The *Gospel according to the Hebrews,* written in the first half of the second century, was for Greek speaking Jewish Christians. It probably originated in Egypt, one reason for believing that was its main witnesses are the Alexandrians, Clement and Origen. The gospel was apparently not a development from any of the four canonical gospels. It contained traditions of Jesus' pre-existence and his coming into the world.

Gospel of the Naassenes. Hippolytus in Book V of his *Refutation of All Heresies* quoted the *Gospel of the Naassenes.* The origin of the Naassenes, or Ophites, i.e., Serpent-Worshipers, remains unknown. However, since they practiced heathen rites, they were heretics by Hippolytus.

Gospel of the Nazaraeans. The *Gospel of the Nazaraeans* appeared in the first half of the second century in Syrian and Jewish Christian circles. It was apparently an Aramaic translation of a Greek form of the Gospel of Matthew. It was first quoted by Hegesippus *ca* 180, and probably originated in Syria.

Gospel of Peter. Coming from the middle of the second century, the *Gospel of Peter* was a development in a Gnostic direction of the four canonical gospels. It was not, however, a full-blown Gnostic work. It was known by reference only (since there were no extant quotations from it) until the winter of 1886-87 when a fragment, coming from the eighth or ninth century, was found at Akhmim in Upper Egypt. The gospel began with Pilate's washing of his hands and ended with a unique description of Jesus' resurrection.

Gospel of Thomas. The *Gospel of Thomas* was a late fourth or early fifth century "gospel," consisting of sayings of Jesus, but with no narrative. It was discovered *ca* 1945 near the village of Nag Hammadi, up the Nile River in Egypt. The sayings, written in Sahidic Coptic, almost certainly originated in Greek, *ca* 140. An early Greek version of some of the sayings appeared in the *Oxyrhynchus Papyrus* fragments.

Hippolytus. Born *ca* 170 CE, Hippolytus spent much of his life in Rome as a presbyter and bishop for about seven years (222 - 23 to 230). He separated from Calixtus who had been elected bishop. He was sent into exile to the mines of Sardinia in 235 and died there or in Rome, probably the following year; he was buried on the road to Tivoli. He wrote many books but was known chiefly for his *Refutation of All Heresies,* which tried to prove that the heresies originated in Greek philosophy and in paganism.

Jerome. Jerome, born in Stridon, Dalmatia, between 331 and 342 CE, was educated in Rome where he was baptized *ca* 370 and later became an ascetic. In 385, he left Rome for Jerusalem where he presided over a monastery until his death in 420. His supreme gift to Christendom was the *Vulgate* - his translation of the whole Bible into Latin. Also of great importance are his many commentaries on biblical books, his dialogue, *Against the Pelagians* in three books (415 CE), and *On Illustrious Men,* written in 392 and 393, which was a list of ecclesiastical writers from the apostles to his own times with their main works. Many of his letters were also preserved.

Josephus. Joseph ben Matthias was born a Jerusalem Jew in 37 or 38 CE and died about 100 CE. At the age of sixteen, he explored the teachings of the Pharisees, the Sadducees, and the Essenes. Still not satisfied he studied under a desert ascetic named Bannus and upon returning to Jerusalem at nineteen, he became a Pharisee and served as a priest until the age of twenty-six. In the next year, he traveled to Rome to free several Jewish priests imprisoned by Felix the procurator of Judah. Through the acquaintance of a Jewish actor, Aliturus, he gained access to the imperial palace and was introduced to Poppaea, Nero's wife, and he was able to secure the release of the priests.

In 64 CE, the Jewish rebellion against Rome was rising, but his own involvement remains uncertain since his accounts of this revolt conflicted with each other. At twenty-nine (66/67) he was in Galilee in command of a Jewish army revolting against Rome and at Jotapata, he surrendered to Vespasian. He was placed under guard for a period in Caesarea, only to later accompany the Roman army to Jerusalem, where he served as an adviser and interpreter for Titus during the siege of the city and the destruction of the temple. He was an eyewitness and participant to many of the events of the Jewish War.

After the war, Josephus took the Roman name Flavius Josephus and accompanied Titus back to Rome where Vespasian gave him an apartment, honored him with Roman citizenship, granted him a pension, and a large tract of land in Judea. At the death of Vespasian, Josephus remained in favor with the two sons, Titus and Domitian, and was provided the freedom to write *The History of the Jewish War* and the *Jewish Antiquities*.

Josephus' writings are important because he was an eyewitness and he presented a different approach from Philo and the authors of 4 Ezra, 2 Baruch and the Apocalypse of Abraham. Yet, as a client of the Roman emperor, he wrote a history that later would be adopted as the empire's authorized version of the events. He did not hesitate to express Titus's goodwill toward the Jewish people and that he wanted to avoid the destruction of the temple. On the other hand, as a Judean he criticized the Judeans who he believed caused the revolt while he praised the virtue of the Jewish religion and God. He justified his desertion of the Jewish cause, and therefore the reader should practice some discrimination. However, Josephus presented an interesting account on the character of Herod the Great, what the temple and Jerusalem looked like in Jesus' days and why the Roman army was so invincible.

Justin. He was called Justin the Martyr from his testimony unto death in Rome *ca* 165 CE. Justin was born in Samaria of non-Christian parents. A student of philosophy, he gradually converted to

Christianity as the oldest, truest and most divine of all philosophies. In its defense, he wrote his *Apology* (for Christianity) *ca* 155, addressed to the Emperor Antoninus Pius and his colleagues; and his *Dialogue with Trypho*, shortly after, which defended Christianity against the attacks of Judaism with a discussion between Justin and a Judean named Trypho.

Mishnah. The Mishnah was essentially a collection of Jewish legal rulings and opinions. The Mishnah was divided into six orders, a structure that both the Babylonian and the Palestinian Talmuds followed. Each order had between seven and twelve subdivisions called tractates (each identified as Mishnah plus name of tractate), which are divided into chapters. It was said that to understand the Mishnah was to understand everything that was done, no matter how mundane, had a spark of the holy within it.

- Zeraim/Seeds dealt with the laws of agriculture.
  - Berakhot – 9 chs on prayers and benedictions.
  - Pe'ah – 8 chs on laws governing charity and gleanings.
  - Demai – 7 chs on doubtfully tithed produce.
  - Kilayim – 9 chs on seeds, trees and animals.
  - Shevi'it – 10 chs on laws of the sabbatical year.
  - Terumot – 11 chs on contributions to the priests.
  - Ma'aserot – 5 chs on tithes for the Levites and the poor.
  - Ma'aser Sheni – 5 chs on second tithe.
  - Khalah – 4 chs on dough offering to the priests.
  - Bikurin – 3 chs on offering of the first fruits.
- Mo'ed/Appointed Seasons covered the laws governing the festivals, fast days and Sabbath.
  - Sabbath – 24 chs of laws governing the Sabbath.
  - Eruvin – 10 chs of laws establishing permissive limits for carrying on Sabbath.
  - Pesakhim – 10 chs to govern the khametz, matzah and the paschal sacrifice.

- Shekalim – 8 chs of laws governing the shekel donation to the Temple.
- Yoma – 8 chs of laws governing Yom Kippur sacrifice and fasting.
- Sukkah – 8 chs of laws governing the building of the sukkah, the Four Species and festival of Sukkot.
- Beitsah – 5 chs of general festival laws.
- Rosh Hashanah – 4 chs on fixing date of the New Year, blowing of the Shofar, Rosh Hashanah prayers.
- To'anit – 4 chs of laws on governing fast days.
- Megillah – 4 chs of laws governing Purim.
- Mo'ed Katan – 3 chs of laws governing intermediate festival days.
- Hagigah – 3 chs of laws concerning the pilgrimage festivals.

- Nashim/Women were primarily concerned with laws governing marriage, divorce, betrothal and adultery. It also contained the Nazirite vows of asceticism.
  - Yebamot – 16 chs of laws on Levirate marriage, prohibited marriages.
  - Ketubot – 13 chs on marriage contracts and agreements.
  - Nazir – 9 chs of laws dealing with the Nazirite laws.
  - Sotah – 9 chs of laws regarding adultery, war and murder in which the perpetrator is unknown.
  - Gittin – 9 chs of laws on divorce and the *get*.
  - Kiddushin – 4 chs of laws on the marriage act, genealogy.

- Nezikin/Damages were concerned with civil and criminal law, including the treatment of idolators and the Pike Avot/ Sayings of the Fathers, a collection of ethical maxims.
  - Baba Kama – 10 chs of laws on direct and indirect damages in civil law.
  - Baba Metzia – 10 chs of laws on losses, loans, work and wage contracts.
  - Baba Batra – 10 chs of laws on partnership, sales, promissory notes, inheritance.

- Sahnedrin – 11 chs of laws regarding the courts, criminal laws, principles of faith.
- Makot – 3 chs of laws regarding punishment by flagellation.
- Shevuot – 8 chs of laws on oaths.
- Eduyot – 8 chs in a collection of testimonies from the sages.
- Avodah Zarah – 5 chs on laws regarding idolators.
- Avot – 5 chs that contain the Sayings "of the Fathers".
- Horayot – 3 chs containing cases involving errors by the court and their correction.

- Kedoshim/Holy Things covered sacrifices, ritual slaughter and the priesthood.
  - Zevahim – 14 chs of laws regarding sacrifice.
  - Menakhot – 13 chs of laws regarding meal offerings.
  - Khulin – 12 chs of laws on ritual slaughter and dietary laws.
  - Bekhorot – 9 chs of laws regarding firstborn child, firstborn animals, defective animals.
  - Arakhin – 9 chs of laws on valuation of Temple offerings and soil.
  - Temurah – 7 chs of laws on substituting an animal offering.
  - Keritot – 6 chs of laws regarding sins requiring expiation.
  - Me'ilah – 6 chs of laws regarding sins of sacrilege against Temple property.
  - Tamid – 7 chs of laws on daily sacrifices in the Temple.
  - Midot – 5 chs of laws regarding measurements of the Temple.
  - Kinim – 3 chs of laws on procedure in the event of mixing sacrifices.

- Tohorot/Purities with a majority of the tractates dealing with the issues of ritual purity and impurity.
  - Kelim – 30 chs of laws regarding utensils and pollution.

- Oholot -18 chs of laws governing the dead and ritual purity.
- Nega'im – 14 chs of laws regarding leprosy.
- Parah – 12 chs of laws regarding the sacrifice of the red heifer, purification after contact with the dead.
- Tohorot – 10 chs of laws of purification.
- Mikva'ot – 10 chs of laws governing the *mikveh* (water and purification before the Sabbath).
- Niddah – 10 chs of laws regarding menstruation and ritual impurity in women.
- Makhshirin – 6 chs of laws concerning ways in which food becomes ritually unclean.
- Zavim – 5 chs of laws regarding gonorrhea and purification.
- Tevul Yom – 4 chs of laws on other types of ritual impurity.
- Yadayim – 4 chs of laws on ritual uncleanliness of the hands.
- Uktsin – 3 chs of laws on things that are susceptible to ritual uncleanliness.

Origen. Origen was born in 184–85 CE, and lived mostly in Alexandria where he headed the catechetical school and in Caesarea where he probably died in 254 during the Decian persecution. He was a great Christian scholar and a most prolific Christian writer of antiquity, having written thousands of scrolls about the length of the gospel of Matthew. He was a biblical critic and exegete, interpreting scripture allegorically. He wrote numerous commentaries and doctrinal works including *On Prayer;* a great apology, *Contra Celsum (Against Celsus)*, which was a defense of Christianity against the attacks of the pagan Celsus; and what may perhaps had been considered Christianity's first systematic theology, *De Principiis* (On First Principles), in four books. He was also the compiler of the famous *Hexapla*, which contained the OT in six columns - the Hebrew, a Greek transliteration of the Hebrew, the Septuagint and the Greek translations of Aquila, Theodotion and Symmachus. This must have been about nine thousand pages long.

Oxyrhynchus Papyrus. This fragment of papyrus, discovered in Oxyrhynchus, Egypt in 1897, probably dated back to the middle of the second century and contained some sayings of Jesus in Greek. The sayings of Jesus found in this document were the same or similar to those found in the Coptic gospel of Thomas found about 1945 at Nag Hammadi. The sayings of Jesus in both these documents were similar, in varying degrees, to those found in the gospels of Matthew, Mark and Luke, but usually represent a later form of the sayings with their own particular characteristics.

Pesikta Rabbati. or P'sqita Rabbita was a collection of Aggadic Midrash (homilies) on the Pentateuchal and prophetic lessons, the special sabbaths, etc. It was composed around 845 CE and probably called *"rabbati"* (the larger) to distinguish it from the earlier Pesikta. The Rabbati contained about fifty-one homilies with seven or eight belonging to Hanukkah, and about seven each to the Feast of Weeks and New Year, while the older Pesiḵta contained one each for Ḥanukkah and the Feast of Weeks and two for New Year.

Philo. Philo of Alexandria (c. 20 BCE - 50 CE), also called Philo Judaeus, was a Hellenistic Jewish philosopher who lived in Alexandria, Egypt during the Roman Empire. In an attempt to harmonize Greek philosophy with Jewish philosophy, he used the allegory approach. While his writings were embraced by several Christian church fathers, it received a less than warm reception within Judaism. Philo believed the literal interpretation of the Hebrew Bible would limit humanity's view and perception of a God too complex and marvelous to be understood in human terms. He maintained that the stories in the Pentateuch (Torah plus Joshua) were elaborate metaphors and symbols and could not be understood as a concrete and objective history. Philo disagreed with the theology that God actively changed the world, was filled with zeal, was moved by repentance, and aided his chosen people. He argued that God existed in neither time nor space and had no human attributes or emotions. Therefore, God had no attributes, in consequence no name, and he could not be perceived by man. Further, God cannot change: He was always the same. He needed no other being and was self-sufficient. God could never perish. He was simply existent and had no relations with any other being.

Some scholars accepted that his concept of the Logos as God's creative principle influenced some of the early Christian writings, while others denied any direct influence and believed that both Philo and early Christianity borrowed from a common unidentified source. The few biographical details known about Philo were found in his own works, especially in *Legatio ad Gaium* [Embassy to Gaius], and in *Josephus*. The only event in his life that could be fixed was his participation in the embassy to Rome in 40 CE. He represented the Alexandrian Jewish view before Roman Emperor Caligula because of civil strife between the Alexandrian Jewish and Greek communities.

Rabbi Akiba. Akiba ben Joseph was a poor, semi-literate shepherd, but Akiba (45-135 CE) became one of Judaism's greatest scholars. He developed the exegetical method of the Mishnah, linking each traditional practice to a basis in the biblical text and systematized the material that later became the Mishnah. Rabbi Akiba was active in the Bar Kokhba rebellion against Rome, 132-135 CE. He believed that Bar Kokhba was the messiah, though some other rabbis openly ridiculed him for that belief. The Talmud recorded another rabbi as saying, "Akiba, grass will grow in your cheeks and still the son of David will not have come." When the Bar Kokhba rebellion failed, Rabbi Akiba was taken by the Roman authorities and tortured to death as he uttered the Sh'ma.

Second Esdras. The book, known as Second Esdras, differed from the other fourteen books in the Apocrypha, because it contained a series of apocalyptic visions from different hands and compiled mostly late in the first or early in the second century after Christ. Second Esdras was included in the Latin Vulgate Bible, except for a missing section (7.36-105) that denied the value of prayers for the dead.

Second Esdras has been ascribed to a certain Salathiel, the father of Zerubbabel, the builder of the second temple. However, Salathiel was identified with Ezra the scribe, who in reality lived during the following century. Evidence lead to the belief that the author was probably a Palestinian Jew who boasted of being a priestly descendent of Aaron and who wrote at the end of the first Christian century, that was approximately thirty years after the destruction of Jerusalem and the temple. In fact, the book contained a lot of NT phraseology. The Second Book of Esdras has been translated into many languages and the Council of Trent placed this book, called the Fourth Book of Esdras as an appendix to the NT.

The purpose of Second Esdras was to denounce the wickedness of Rome, to grieve about what had happened to Jerusalem, and to wrestle with a perplexing religious question about God, and the evils of society. The fall of Jerusalem and the temple placed a great strain on the Jewish faith. How do you reconcile God's justice, wisdom, power and goodness with all of the evil things that have happened to them?

Second Esdras remains a difficult book to read in our time, because we do not care for or understand his elaborate use of symbolism from the seven visions. However, he dealt with some critical issues related to both the Jewish people and Christians. A disturbed Ezra mourned the destruction of Jerusalem and set about to explain the problem of evil (3.1-5.20). Since Adam, humanity possessed a tendency to sin, and yet the Creator had not removed this tendency even from his chosen people. Rather, God, the Most High, held them responsible for their deeds and punished them at the hands of the Gentiles, whose deeds were worse than those of the Jewish people. The response was a series of riddles or questions that were not answered, but with the assertion that the ways of the Most High were beyond human capacity (4.13-21). Ezra was not interested in understanding heavenly things; he wanted to know what God was going to do about the suffering of Israel under the hands of the Gentiles (4.22-25).

He then turned to the end of time and wondered why God could not have arranged things in order that the end would come sooner. The answer was that God's time is appropriate to the nature of things and Ezra was commanded to fast for another seven days (5.31-6.35).

The question was presented that if God created the world for Israel, why has Israel been dominated by the nations and how long will it continue? Ezra wanted to know about God's justice (6.36-9.36). The hope for an age to come was fine for the righteous (Israel), but what about the wicked (Gentiles), who could anticipate only punishment? The response was that God gave the covenant and the Torah, and all would be judged according to their deeds. Then a description of the last days was given with a four-hundred year reign of the Messiah, before the resurrection and the great judgment over which God would preside. Judgment would be based on deeds, and even the Gentiles would be punished for not having served the Most High and obeyed the commandments.

Ezra wanted to know who among the living had not sinned. The question was dismissed and God would not grieve over the many that would perish (7.45-74) along with a contrast between hell and paradise (7.75-101). Ezra wanted to know if the wicked might be saved at the judgment through the intercession of the righteous (7.102-3), and with the negative answer learned that life was a contest in which people must make the choice (7.104-140). The world was made for many, but the age to come for the sake of only a few (8.1-3). Ezra pleaded for mercy and received assurance he was among the righteous, and the discussion about the many that would perish ended (8.4-8.47).

The fourth vision was a woman who represented the heavenly Zion and mourned over the death of her son (9.26-10.59). The fifth was the Eagle, used to describe the Roman Empire that was defeated by the lion, the Messiah (11.1-12.39). The sixth vision was a reference to the Messiah and the ten lost tribes of Israel (13.1-58), and the final vision was that God addressed Ezra while he was sitting under an oak tree, telling him that the end was near, and he was to produce ninety-four books within a forty-day period (14.1-48). Still, the editor had a strong religious faith, and in spite of all that has happened, he sought to justify the ways of God to man.

Tertullian. Quintus Septimius Florens Tertullianus, better known as Tertullian, was born in Carthage, in the Roman providence of Africa *ca* 150-55. He studied law and converted to Christianity *ca* 190-95. He has been called "the father of Latin Christianity." He broke with the "Catholic" Church *ca* 207 in favor of the asceticism of the Montanists. He was perhaps most famous for being the first to use the term "Trinity" (Latin trinitas), giving rise to a formal exposition of a Trinitarian theology. In his work there appeared "three Persons, one Substance" as the Latin "tres Personae, una Substantia." His Trinitarian formula was presented after he became a Montanist and therefore, his ideas were at first rejected as heresy by the church at large, only to be later embraced as Christian doctrine. When he died *ca* 223, he had left the Montanists and founded a sect of his own. His chief polemical work was *Against Marcion* in five books written over a period of about twelve years, 200-12.

Testament of the Twelve Patriarchs. This is a pseudepigraphic work from 200 BCE to 200 CE to have contained the deathbed speeches of the twelve sons of Jacob. The Testaments of Asher, Benjamin, Daniel, Issachar, Judah, Levi, and Naphtali are referenced in the notes on Mt 8.29 and Mark 5.7.

Tobit. The book of Tobit was named after a generous and God-fearing Jewish man whose blindness and poverty in Nineveh resulted directly from his performing one of his most characteristic good deeds burying an executed fellow-Judean. Thanks to the courageous efforts of his devoted son, Tobias, who was assisted by the angel Raphael, disguised as Azariah, Tobit not only recovered his sight and fortune but also gained a pious daughter-in-law, Sarah. From her, Tobias exorcised Amadeus, the demon who had claimed the lives of her seven previous husbands on their wedding nights. On his deathbed, Tobit had Tobias promise to move the family from Nineveh to Ecbatana, where Tobias lived to a rich old age.

The author used three well-known secular folktales: (1) the tale of the Grateful Dead (the story about a man impoverished but ultimately rewarded for burying an abused corpse); (2) the tale of the Monster in the Bridal Chamber (the story of a demon who killed the bride's husbands on their wedding nights); and (3) the tale of Ahiqar (the account of a wise courtier who, though falsely incriminated by his adopted son, was vindicated).

The author of Tobit was a Judean, writing originally in Hebrew or Aramaic (copies in those languages have been found at Qumran), probably somewhere between 225-175 BCE, and, possibly, in Palestine. Tobit was represented by three major Greek recensions and two Latin translations. Unlike the RSV, the NRSV of Tobit was based upon the Sinaiticus family as supplemented by the Old Latin. There were also some late Hebrew translations, which were based upon a Greek text, as were the older Syriac, Ethiopic and Sahidic versions.

Textual Variants in Manuscripts.

Today differing biblical translations continue to increase almost daily and it is left to the reader to determine which interpretation of the text closer represents the intent of the author or the tradition of the faith community. Yet, it seems strange to understand that manuscripts were copied by hand from another manuscript. This meant that every copied manuscript might contain errors, either intentional or unintentional by a scribe who probably worked at this sacred task at a center of learning or monastery. The issue became more complicated as a manuscript was used at a different center of learning became the original for making other copies. Therefore, copies that contained different variants would be copied that would include some of the differing variants in future copies. All of this took place even before the translation of the copies into differing languages. Scholars have long recognized that many manuscripts of the NT could be categorized as families or types of texts usually copied at a specific center of learning. While the number of variants between the differing texts was in the thousands, it was estimated that ninety percent of the NT manuscripts agreed, and the differing variants became the center of our religious debates and discussions. In many of the version of the Bible these different manuscripts were noted as "other ancient authorities" with no additional information. Several of the major families of manuscripts are examined below.

- **Alexandrian Text.** Identified by the location of the center of learning, the Alexandrian Text (called *"Neutral"*) were known for its absence of variants or errors, and these manuscripts included Codex Sinaiticus and Vaticanus, both from the fourth century.

- **Byzantine Text.** This third century text was also called Syrian, Antiochene, Koine and Received (*Texus Receptus*) and was centered around Antioch. These manuscripts were adopted in Constantinople and dominated the Byzantine world. The received text became the basis for the first printed editions of the Greek NT in the sixteenth century. The King James Version was a translation of this type of text. By the eighth century it was the preferred Greek text used and was characterized by its combinations of readings from other manuscripts and revisions that favored smoothness and intelligibility.

- **Caesarean Text.** This text was used in Caesarea, but the discovery of a third century text in Egypt that used this type of text raised the probability it originated in Egypt, perhaps as early as the second century as an Alexandrian text.

- **Syriac Text.** This text, different from the Syrian (Byzantine), was once believed to belong to the Western text, but now most scholars consider it an independent text closer to the Alexandrian text. This text was later revised under the Byzantine influence and became the Peshitta version that became the Bible of the Syrian church.

- **Western Text.** The term "Western text" once referred to all pre-Byzantine, non-Alexandrian manuscripts, but it more properly identified Graeco-Latin manuscripts from Western Europe, such as Codex Bezae and Old Latin versions. This family of texts was noted for their omissions and insertions that sometimes included several verses in length. The text was believed to have originated in the middle of the second century, probably in North Africa or Egypt in Greek. The Western text was translated into Latin rather early. The issue of omissions and insertions gave question to the authenticity of the manuscripts.
- **Community Rule** - Originally known as *The Manual of Discipline,* the Community Rule in the Dead Sea Scrolls contained a set of regulations ordering the life of the members of the "yahad," the group within the Judean Desert sect who chose to live communally and whose members accepted strict rules of conduct. This fragment cited the admonitions and punishments to be imposed on violators of the rules, the method of joining the group, the relationships between the members, their way of life and their beliefs. The sect divided humanity between the righteous and the wicked and asserted that human nature and everything that happens in the world was irrevocably predestined. The scroll ended with songs of praise to God.

  A complete copy of the scroll, eleven columns in length, was found in Cave 1. Ten fragmentary copies were recovered in Cave 4, and a small section was found in Cave 5. The large number of manuscript copies attested to the importance of this text for the sect. This particular fragment was the longest of the versions of this text found in Cave 4.

Versions of the New Testament

Most of the early church read what was to become the NT in either the Hebrew or Greek languages; but when the Gospel message reached those not reading or speaking Hebrew or Greek, it had to be translated into the language of its new hearers. Three of these early translations considered major "versions" were the Coptic (Sahidic and Bohairic), the Latin and the Syriac. Other versions of less value from a textual point of view included the Ethiopic, the Gothic, the Armenian, the Georgian, the Arabic, the Slavonic and the Persian.

Coptic Versions. After the NT spread to the Greek-speaking people in Egypt, it was then shared with the natives who spoke Coptic in various dialects, the Bohairic and the Sahidic.

- **The Bohairic** - The Bohairic or Memphitic version, the only Coptic version to include the complete NT, was current in Lower (northern) Egypt. Bohairic, the most developed of Egyptian dialects, ultimately superseded all other dialects, until *"Coptic"* came to mean *"Bohairic."* Over a hundred manuscripts, all late, have been found. Three date from the twelfth century; the oldest, containing the gospels, was at Oxford and is dated 1173–74 CE. The remaining manuscripts were later; but a single leaf of Ephesians may have been dated in the fifth century. The text was mainly Alexandrian, and the version was dated in the first half of the third century, a little after the Sahidic.
- **The Sahidic** - The Sahidic or Thebaic version was current in Upper (southern) Egypt whose chief city was Thebes, and this version was not known to exist until the end of the eighteenth century. It was found only in numerous fragments from which, however, most of the NT can be put together. Many fragments date from the fifth century, some from the fourth. The text was preponderantly Alexandrian but contained some Western readings, especially in Mark and Luke. The version was dated early in the third century.

Latin Versions. The Latin versions were divided into two groups, the Itala and the Vulgate. The Itala (also known as the Old Latin) referred to all the Old Latin manuscripts not derived from Jerome's Latin translation known as the Vulgate. Jerome indicated that Pope Victor (*ca* 190) was the first person to write theological treatises in Latin. Tertullian, who also wrote in Latin, died around 223. However, as Latin emerged as the language of the Roman Empire, the NT had to be translated into that language.

- **Itala** or **Old Latin** Versions. These manuscripts were divided into three groups: the African manuscripts, the European manuscripts and the Italic manuscripts. Jerome probably took the latter group as the basis for his own revision, and it may have been a modification of the European manuscripts. The African manuscripts were extremely important because they contained the same type of text used in Africa by Tertullian and Cyprian in the second and third centuries. Parts of the gospels then could be recovered in a Latin text from the second century. For translators to recover the Greek text from the Latin, it must be retranslated back into Greek, and before this could be done, a judgment had to be made if the Latin was translated from the Greek literally or in paraphrase. If the translation was from a Latin paraphrase to Greek, the result would not have enabled us to get very close to the original Greek. Also, it must have been decided if the given Latin manuscript was a translation of a Greek manuscript, or the edition of another Latin manuscript. This identified some of the difficulties found in all the versions, be they Latin, Syriac, Coptic or whatever.
- **Vulgate.** In 383, Jerome wrote in the preface to his Latin text of the gospels he had compiled one Latin text because of the great number of Latin texts present that differed both among themselves and from the Greek manuscripts. Jerome's contemporary, Augustine, in his *De Doctrina Christiana,* confirmed the existence of a wide variety of Latin interpretations. Pope Damasus, in order to present the church with what he considered the best available Latin text

and to eliminate from the Latin NT the differing readings, requested that Jerome publish his edition of the gospels in 383, with the rest of the Bible being completed in 405. By the eighth century, Jerome's edition of the Bible became standard in the Roman Catholic Church.

It remains uncertain if Vulgate of the Acts, the Epistles and the Apocalypse go back to Jerome. The earlier Latin manuscripts, included a great variety of readings called the Itala or the Old Latin. There were no complete Bibles in the Old Latin, but only groups of books or fragments that dated from the fourth to the thirteenth centuries. Quotations from the Itala and even entire chapters were found in the writings of the Latin church fathers.

It is unclear what Greek manuscripts Jerome used, but they were apparently of an Alexandrian rather than a Western type. As the years continued, Jerome's Vulgate manuscript itself became corrupt as it was made to conform to the influences of the Old Latin manuscripts that refused to die. Today, there exists scarcely an Old Latin reading that cannot be found in some manuscript of the Vulgate.

Numerous commentators who preferred the Itala and its many surviving manuscripts testified to its use for centuries after Jerome made his great revision. It was still used in Bohemia at the close of the Middle Ages. Because the Vulgate was corrupted by the Old Latin and by many "improvements," it therefore had to be revised. This was undertaken as early as the sixth century by Cassiodorus. Later Charlemagne, aware of the confusion of texts in his day, asked an Englishman, Alcuin, Abbot of St. Martin at Tours, to revise the Latin Bible; and on Christmas day in the year 801, Alcuin presented the Emperor with his revision. Other revisions followed and finally Pope Sixtus V (1585-90) published a text in 1590, accompanied by a bull (document) declaring it alone to be trustworthy. Three months later he died. The College of Cardinals then called in all copies of the Sixtine edition, that contained many errors, and in 1592 Pope Clement VIII (1592-1605) issued his own edition of the Vulgate (the Clementine Vulgate), but under the names of both Sixtus and Clement. The bull that accompanied Clement's Vulgate established it as the standard Roman text, and the third edition of the *Clementina* of 1598 was still the official Latin text of the Bible of the Roman Catholic Church. No verses were to be altered and no variant readings were to be placed in the margin, so that officially, at any rate, textual criticism within the Roman Church was apparently proscribed from that date.

No version of the NT has been so influential and significant in the Western church as the Vulgate. The Vulgate version of the Bible was read throughout Western Europe for a thousand years; and the Vulgate version was carried by missionaries throughout the world and later translated into the vernacular of those receiving the gospel. The first complete book to be printed from a press in Europe was a text of the Vulgate, published in 1455 at Mainz by Gutenberg and Fust. The first complete English Bible was a translation from the Vulgate, made by Wycliffe; it was in the Vulgate version that the present chapter divisions of the Bible were worked out, probably by Stephen Langton, later Archbishop of Canterbury, *ca* 1228.

- **Syriac Versions.** Just as in the Latin where there was an old version (the Old Latin manuscripts) and an authorized version (the Vulgate versions), so in the Syriac there was an old version (the Old Syriac, represented by two manuscripts) and an authorized version (the Peshitta, the common language version).

  - In the eighteenth century, the Peshitta was the only Syriac text known; but scholars like Griesbach felt certain that an Old Syriac text lay behind it. This Old Syriac text was represented by two manuscripts discovered since Griesbach's time, the Curetonian and the Sinaitic Syriac (sy^c and sy^s). In 1842, a Syriac manuscript of the

Gospels arrived at the British Museum from the library of a monastery in the Nitrian Desert in Egypt. William Cureton, the English Syriac scholar and an officer of the Museum, edited the leaves and later published them in 1858, known today by his name. They came from the middle of the fifth century and Dr. Cureton questioned if they contained the words of Jesus just as he spoke them, language and all! He stated that the original of his version was made before the original of the Peshitta. This was hotly disputed by advocates of the Peshitta, but it has since been generally recognized to be true.

○ A second aid in getting at the Old Syriac text was made available in 1836 when the Armenians of the Mechitarist Monastery of San Lazzaro, Venice, published a commentary on Tatian's *Diatessaron* by Ephraem, the Syrian Father of the fourth century that they possessed in an Armenian translation. This was not widely known until 1876, but since then Zahn and others have reconstructed the text on which this commentary, originally in Syriac, was based. Besides the commentary, an Arabic translation of the *Diatessaron* was found in the Vatican Library; and after that, still another Arabic translation was found in Egypt. From these two manuscripts, the *Diatessaron* was edited in 1888. One should not leave the *Diatessaron* without also mentioning the Dura Fragment, which was found on the site of Dura-Europos, a Roman fortified city captured by the Persians in 256 CE. One of the vellum fragments from this site proved to be fourteen imperfect lines of the **Diatessaron** in Greek. Scholars are still uncertain whether Tatian wrote his **Diatessaron** in Greek or in Syriac. There was an Arabic translation that included a Syriac commentary of it in Armenian and a Greek translation, in Mesopotamia, in the early third century.

- **Sinaitic Syriac Version.** Finally, in 1892, two Cambridge women, Mrs. A.S. Lewis and her sister, Mrs. M.D. Gibson, discovered some palimpsest leaves of a Syriac manuscript of the gospels in the same monastery of St. Catherine on Mount Sinai where Tischendorf had found his great Greek uncial, "Sinaiticus." The gospel text underlay of a Syriac treatise dated in the year 778 and was itself of the early fifth century. It was later photographed at Sinai and the photographs were published in 1894 containing about three-fourths of the gospels. Known as Sinaitic Syriac, the manuscript is still at Sinai, and along with other manuscripts there have been rephotographed by an expedition from the American Schools of Oriental Research at Jerusalem.

- **Old Syriac Version.** This Latin version probably originated in the late second century or early third and was akin to the text of Sinaiticus and Vaticanus, with Western readings inserted under the influence of the *Diatessaron.* Some have observed that the two manuscripts do not represent exactly the same text. There were a great deal more differences between them than there were, for instance, between two copies of the Peshitta; and of the two manuscripts, the Sinaitic Syriac represented the earlier text. It was the oldest text of the Syriac that was known. Only the gospels survive in the Old Syriac version; the rest of the NT first appeared in the Syriac language in the Peshitta.

- **Peshitta Version.** While its origin was not certain, the Peshitta (common language) version of the Syriac NT was increasingly used in the Syrian church from the end of the fifth century. Until recently, it was generally believed the Peshitta was edited under the direction of Rabbula, Bishop of Edessa in 411–435, but perhaps it existed before Rabbula, originating in Antioch as an attempt to make the Syriac text conform more closely to the Greek.

The Peshitta remains the basis of the authorized Syriac text today. It has two early, significant revisions, one by Philoxenus, Bishop of Mabug (Hierapolis), in 508, known as the Philoxenian Syriac; and the other by Thomas of Harkel (Heraclea) at Alexandria, in 616, known as the Harclean Syriac.

Additional Reading

Barnstone, Willis & Meyer, Marvin, ed., *The Gnostic Bible,* Boston & London, New Seeds, 2006.

Barrett, C. K., *The New Testament Background*, New York, Harper and Row Publishers, 1961.

Bevan, Edwyn, *Jerusalem Under the High-Priests*, Edward Arnold and Co., London, 1940.

Burrows, Millar, *The Dead Sea Scrolls*, New York, Gramercy Publishing Company, 1986.

Burton, Ernest DeWitt, and Goodspeed, Edgar Johnson, *A Harmony of the Synoptic Gospels,* New York, Charles Scribner's Sons, 1945.

Buttrick, George A., Editor, *The Interpreter's Dictionary of the Bible*, Four Volumes, Nashville, Abingdon Press, 1986.

Buttrick, George A., Editor, *The Interpreter's Bible, A Commentary in Twelve Volumes*, Nashville, Abingdon Press, 1957.

Crossan, John Dominic, *The Birth of Christianity,* San Francisco, Ca., Harper Collins Publisher, 1998.

Cullmann, Oscar, *The Christology of the New Testament,* Philadelphia, The Westminster Press, 1963.

Davies, W. D., *Introduction to Pharisaism*, Philadelphia, Fortress Press, 1967.

Dupont-Sommer, A., *The Essene Writings from Qumran*, New York, The World Publishing Co., 1967.

Eisenman, Robert, *The Dead Sea Scrolls and the First Christians*, New York, Barnes & Noble Books, 2004.

Ellis, E. Earle, *Eschatology in Luke*, Biblical Series, Facet Books, Philadelphia, Pa., Fortress Press, 1972.

Forester, Werner, *From Exile to Christ*, Philadelphia, Fortress Press, 1964.

Fuller, Reginald, *Interpreting the Miracles*, Philadelphia, The Westminster Press, 1963.

Goodacre, Mark S., *The Case Against Q: Studies in Marken Priority and the Synoptic_Problem*, Harrisburg, Pennsylvania, Trinity Press International, 2002.

Gaster, Theodor H., *The Dead Sea Scriptures*, Garden City, New York, Doubleday & Co., 1976.

Hunter, Archibald M., *The Work and Words of Jesus*, Philadelphia, The Westminster Press, 1950.

Jeffers, James S., *The Greco-Roman World of the New Testament Era*, Downers Grove, Illinois, InterVarsity Press, 1999.

Jeremias, Jochim, *Rediscovering the Parables*, New York, Charles Scribner's Sons, 1966.

Josephus, *Thrones of Blood, A History of the Times of Jesus 37 BC to A.D. 70*, A Barbour Book, 1988.

Major, H. D. A., Manson, T.W., Wright, C. J., *The Mission and Message of Jesus*, New York, E. P. Dutton and Co., Inc., 1961.

Mack, Burton L., *The Lost Gospel the Book of Q & Christian Origins*, San Francisco, Harper, 1993.

Manson, T. W., *Only to the House of Israel*, Philadelphia, Fortress Press, 1964.

Manson, T. W., *The Servant-Messiah*, Grand Rapids, Michigan, Baker Book House, 1977.

Metzger, Bruce M., and Murphy, Roland E., Editors, "Matthew," *The New Oxford Annotated Bible with the Aprocryphal/Deuterocanonical Books*, New Revised Standard Version, New York, New York, Oxford University Press, 1994.

Moule, C. F. D., *The Birth of the New Testament, third ed.*, San Francisco, Harper & Row Publishers, 1982.

Niebuhr, H. Richard, *Christ and Culture*, Philadelphia, Harper Torchbooks, 1965.

North, Christopher R., *The Suffering Servant in Duetero-Isaiah*, London, Oxford, Press, 1969.

Pfeiffer, Robert H., *History of the New Testament Times*, New York, Harper and Brothers, 1949.

Reicke, Bo, *The New Testament Era*, Philadelphia, Fortress Press, 1968.

Robinson, J.A.T., *Jesus and His Coming*, Nashville, Abingdon Press, 1957.

Robinson, James M., Editor, *The Sayings Gospel Q in Greek and English*, Minneapolis, Fortress Press, 2002.

Russell, D. S., *The Jews from Alexander to Herod*, New York, Oxford University Press, 1975.

Sanders, James A., *Torah and Canon*, Philadelphia, Fortress Press, 1972.

Saunders, Ernest W., *Jesus in the Gospels*, Englewood Cliffs, N. J., Prentice-Hall, Inc., 1967.

Westerman, Claus, *The Old Testament and Jesus Christ*, Minneapolis, Minnesota, Augsburg Publishing House, 1968.

Wise, Michael; Abegg, Martin, and Cook, Edward, *The Dead Sea Scrolls, A New Translation*, San Francisco, Harper, 1996.

Cast Index

Printed in the United States
By Bookmasters